Good News
About Your
Strong-Willed
Child

Good News
About Your
Strong-Willed Child

Understanding and Raising
the Child Who Opposes You

Randy Reynolds
with Paul Moede

ZondervanPublishingHouse
Grand Rapids, Michigan

A Division of HarperCollinsPublishers

Good News About Your Strong-Willed Child
Copyright © 1995 by Randy Reynolds

Requests for information should be addressed to:
Zondervan Publishing House
Grand Rapids, Michigan 49530

Library of Congress Cataloging-in-Publication Data

Reynolds, Randy.
  Good news about your strong-willed child : understanding and raising
the child who opposes you / Randy Reynolds with Paul Moede.
      p.   cm.
    ISBN: 0-310-48611-4 (softcover)
    1. Problem children.   2. Child rearing.   I. Moede, Paul.   II. Title.
HQ773.R49   1994
649'.1—dc20   94-48420
                                                                      CIP

Edited by Jeron Frame
Interior design by Joe Vriend

Printed in the United States of America

95 96 97 98 99 00 / ❖ DH / 10 9 8 7 6 5 4 3 2 1

This book is dedicated to my wife,
Lynn Marry Reynolds,
who encourages and allows me to fulfill my dreams,
which are often at her expense.

Contents

Acknowledgments

There are many people who have contributed to making this book possible. Paul Moede, who worked with me on this book, was invaluable as he took abstract concepts and built them into a coherent and enjoyable manuscript. Both Paul and I are thankful for Sandy VanderZicht, our editor, who has been both supportive and very helpful in this project, and to Jeron Frame for her editorial expertise.

I feel a debt of gratitude to the therapists in the field of marriage and family who have written extensively about how families work and do not work at times. I especially appreciate Dr. Murray Bowen's work with families. I am thankful to Dr. Carol Evans for her training of counselors in the area of family systems.

I appreciate the opportunity to work with hurting families over the years who have encouraged me and allowed me to see the dynamics of the concepts in this book in their lives. I have been enriched by the changes and adjustments they have made. I have been inspired by their pain and hard work to write about them and their progress.

I am also thankful to Renewal Counseling, the staff, board members, and donors for their continued encouragement and support. Without them this book would be impossible. This is especially true with Becky DeVoe, our office manager, who has played a major role in getting this book finished.

I also acknowledge that without God's blessing and Christ's compassion for the wounded this book would not have been written.

Introduction

This book isn't about the little child who occasionally yells a defiant, No!

It's about the child whose whole attitude toward life seems to scream out, No!

This book deals with the strong-willed child: the problem kid who gives his parents fits, the child who doesn't seem to mesh with the family system, the one who doesn't seem to buy its system of values, standards, and beliefs. Over time, he gets labeled the "bad kid," and parents assume he's the problem in the family.

But that assumption contributes to the dilemma. The strong-willed child is part of the family, not separate from it. She affects the family and the family affects her. Unfortunately, most of the time she feels like an alien. She wishes her family would leave her alone, and they wish she would be less of a problem. But unless the two get together—unless every member of the family learns the part he or she plays in the family's difficulties—the dilemma will never be solved.

I believe this is a unique approach which most Christian books on the strong-willed child do not address. In my work with families, particularly those with difficult children, I have found that the strong-willed child's behavior is both a cause and an effect of the family's relational problems. A child makes an unreasonable demand, causing a parent to react in anger, which in turn causes the child to lash out. Unless the parent recognizes his own role in this cycle and steps out of it, the cycle will continue.

There are many handbooks out there that give parents tips for "handling" their strong-willed child. If you are looking for a handbook of easy answers, a tried-and-true list of parenting methods, you will not find it here.

What you will find, however, is freedom: the freedom to "unlabel" your child, the freedom to understand the underlying emotional system of your family, and the freedom to break the chains that bind your family in unhealthy relationships.

Many of you with a strong-willed child feel that life is hopeless. You marvel at your friends' reasonable and rational children, and you envy them their pleasant family outings and their warm and intimate conversations. You wonder what you've done wrong to produce a child who fights you at every turn. You may even have resigned yourself to simply surviving the next few years until your child is grown and gone.

It doesn't have to be this way. God created your family to be a unique entity. Each member reflects his image—strong-willed, compliant, and everything in between. By working together to accept each other and to respond to each other in healthy, productive ways, you can realize his will for your family.

Your strong-willed child will probably never be "cured." But in writing this book, I hope to help you modify your style of parenting so that it becomes part of the solution, not part of the problem. Eventually the strong-willed "piece" in your family "puzzle" will find a perfect fit.

Chapter One

My Child Versus
the Good Child

A wise son brings joy to his father,
but a foolish son grief to his mother.
Proverbs 10:1

WHY IS EVERYONE HAVING SUCH A BAD DAY?

Sarah stumbled from the shower and drank in the rich aroma of steaming coffee wafting up from the kitchen. Rob was enjoying his first cup, and after Sarah was assured that Teddy and Peter were getting ready for school, she would be enjoying hers too.

13

"Morning, Mom!" Peter said as he bounded up the stairway to his room.

His greeting was as dependable as the sunrise. He was already dressed, had eaten breakfast, and was on his way to pack his backpack.

"Mornin', hon," Sarah replied with an easy smile.

She could always count on Peter. What more could a mother ask for in a firstborn son? It was hard to believe that he was already ten.

Sarah slipped her head through the partially open door of Teddy's room. Across the floor cluttered with toys and next to the dresser with clothes hanging out of every drawer, Teddy sat half upright in his bed.

"Mornin', sweetheart!" Sarah said. "Time to get going or you'll be late for the school bus. Don't let Monday slow you down."

Teddy turned his head, and the squint in his eyes let Sarah know that her schedule was not going to be his.

"It ain't Monday," Teddy snapped irritably.

Sarah's stomach tightened. If there was going to be an early morning confrontation, she instinctively knew that this was the room from which it would come. She dreaded another morning of battle with her seven-year-old. Her bright morning greeting took a more serious tone.

"Teddy, I'm not going to argue with you today," she said sternly. "It's Monday, the bus comes in forty-five minutes, and you're going to be ready for it."

Sarah pulled back and saw Peter in his room, packing up his homework. If only Teddy could be half as obedient as Peter, she thought. Peter made her feel so good about being a parent. He always seemed to know the right thing to do. When conflicts arose with Teddy, he would go out of his way to keep peace in the house. She felt that she treated them both the same, so what made Peter such a good boy and Teddy—well, what made him so different?

"Yo, Mom!" Peter yelled down the hallway. "I spent my lunch money on some very hot, new edition baseball cards. Can you give me a few extra dollars for lunch?"

"Sure. Take it out of my purse on the dresser," Sarah replied with a smile of playful exasperation.

Peter's money was supposed to cover lunches for the next two days, she remembered. But Peter was basically a good kid, and a little financial irresponsibility could be easily ignored.

"If it's Monday, why does it feel like Saturday?" Teddy yelled from behind his partially closed bedroom door.

Sarah pivoted abruptly in the hall and mentally drew a line in the sand. Last night Teddy had continually poked and teased Peter at the dinner table until Sarah exploded. She was sick and tired of his constant pushing and rebellion. All through dinner she cast hot glances at Rob, signaling him to step in and take charge. But Rob saw the humor in some of Teddy's barbs and so he "rolled with the punches." But that was just like Teddy, she thought, mixing just enough humor and charm with a belligerent attitude to avoid discipline from his father. It didn't help that Rob was so easygoing. Even now she was imagining how tired she would be if she had to battle Teddy alone. Not today, she vowed to herself. Not today.

Sarah wheeled back into Teddy's room with a determination and speed that surprised her. Teddy hadn't moved an inch.

"Teddy, if you think I'm going to waste my time in some stupid debate with a know-it-all second-grader, you're sorely mistaken!" Sarah shouted. "I don't need you or anybody else in this house to tell me how things are going to be. You got that? And another thing, you can forget playing over at Sean's house after school. You're grounded!"

Teddy actually looked shocked, an emotion that didn't often surface for Sarah to see.

"But, Mom, I . . ." Teddy began.

"No!" Sarah interrupted. "There's nothing I want to hear from you."

Of course, there were many things that Sarah longed to hear. "Please" and "thank you" would be nice. A voice that didn't always whine or challenge would be wonderful. Or just a simple "okay" when she asked Teddy to do the smallest thing. There were many things Sarah longed to hear from this child who held so much promise if he could channel his energy in positive directions.

Sarah stomped into the bathroom and began to slap on her makeup. She was committed to winning this conflict with Teddy. Unfortunately, Sarah didn't feel like a winner at all. Not after what she said and especially how she said it. Her makeup was covering her face but it wasn't doing a thing for her feelings of guilt.

Monday morning in the Townsend household. Maybe it's just like yours. The presence of a strong-willed child like Teddy can make parenting—already a difficult challenge—into a daily struggle for power. Perpetual conflicts, bitter words, and frustrated attempts at discipline send the whole family into a downward-spinning spiral.

In your home this child may be called Jeffrey or Todd; she may be called Jennifer or Kristi. Whatever the name, he or she is the strong-willed child, the one who opposes you as parent and leader. This child may oppose you all the time, or he may be going through an "oppositional phase." Whatever the duration, these contrary behaviors can hook the whole family into conflict—each member playing his or her own unique role to keep conflict boiling on the burner.

The strong-willed child acts out more than normally rebellious children and teens who are seeking to test the limits of parental boundaries. The strong-willed child continually and forcefully opposes those in authority. She constantly challenges parental value systems and, depending upon the severity of the challenge, will tyrannize and embarrass her parents. Parenting becomes an overwhelming challenge, and family unity a dream.

As conflicts continue, children in opposition can cause parents to conclude that they are totally inadequate for parenting. These negative emotions eat away at parental self-worth. Ultimately, many parents of strong-willed children are forced to seek outside help from family, friends, or professional counselors. The child who once rested snugly in their arms now seems to have one overriding ambition: to show Mom and Dad how little they know about being a parent. The strong-willed child is hooked into conflict with parents, who in turn are hooked into conflict with the child.

If you have a strong-willed child, you may feel like you're the only one who gets regular calls from the school office or endures disapproving glares from other parents at church socials. You may not be able to remember the last time you found shopping enjoyable or spent an untainted evening with your spouse. And worst of all, you may be secretly wondering what you did or didn't do that made your child so relentlessly unreasonable and rebellious.

You are not alone. Many parents struggle with and feel defeated by their strong-willed children. In this book you will read the stories of parents who, like you, wake every morning to a potential battlefield. Some of these parents are still struggling. But many have taken positive steps toward breaking the cycles of conflict.

The Conforming Child and the Strong-Willed Child

The Townsend boys provide a good illustration of the differences between strong-willed children and their opposites, children who conform. Examine the following list of behaviors for the opposing and the conforming child to see where your children fall. Keep in mind that these behaviors are not mutually exclusive, nor are they cast in concrete. A strong-willed child will have positive characteristics, and a conforming child will have negative characteristics. Most children, however, will tend to lean decisively toward one of these two behavior patterns. Which of the two characterizes your child?

Strong-Willed Child
Argumentative
Strong-willed
Anger that covers sadness

Conforming Child
Reasonable
Yielding
Sadness that covers anger

Blames others	Takes responsibility
Fighter	Lover
Opposes the rules	Conforms to the rules
Ruled by feelings	Ruled by reason and thought
Assertive	Tentative
Self-sensitive	Sensitive to others
Negative outlook	Positive outlook
Always demands fairness	Accepts that life isn't always fair
Disruptive	Cooperative
Reactive	Responsive
Disrespectful	Respectful
Feels weak, acts powerful	Feels weak, acts weak

I suspect that if you had a choice, there wouldn't be much doubt about which type of child you'd pick to be your own! But that's exactly the problem. If you picked the conforming child, you have made some firm but potentially damaging conclusions. It's tempting to conclude that the conforming child is the "good child" and the strong-willed child is the "bad child." This assessment is based on personality type instead of heart attitudes and personal strengths.

When you assign "good" and "bad" labels to your child, you also tend to adopt communication tactics that match the label. Frequently a parent will respond to the conforming child in positive, affirming ways because the child reflects their values and viewpoints. With the opposing child, however, the parent will react with less positive communication. Sarah Townsend dismissed her conforming son's irresponsibility with money because he was "basically a good kid." But she launched into an immediate tirade with her younger, strong-willed son because, based on past experiences, she "knew" he was going to be difficult that morning.

Many parents are frustrated because they don't recognize that they must parent the conforming child and the strong-willed child differently. If you stand up to a conforming child, he usually obeys. If you challenge a strong-willed child, however, he will probably oppose you even more. Strong-willed children are more work to parent, but that does not mean that they are bad children. Their opposition can reveal to us the changes we need to make in parenting.

The Family As a System

The strong-willed child is not an entity unto herself. She—and her parents—are part of the organic system that we call the family.

The family system is comprised of family members and their values, beliefs, rules, role, and dynamics. This system is not static. It goes through changes that place strains on its individual members. When a strong-willed child reacts against her family or circumstances, the entire system is impacted. Power struggles lead to reactions and responses from other family members, and soon behaviors and beliefs become lifelong patterns. Consider the case of the Smalls.

Robert Small was a college professor who placed a high priority on education. More than that, he demanded that his three sons excel in academics. Byron and Christopher met their father's expectations and, for the most part, were pleasing in his eyes. His middle son, Jim, however, refused to maintain his father's intense standards. The constant push for achievement and the unrelenting pressure for competitive grades exasperated him. Jim obstinately pursued his own path, working with his hands rather than slaving over books, in part to spite his father.

When Jim's grades fell, his father exploded. He humiliated him in front of his brothers and wrote Jim off as a failure. Jim was angry, but also painfully aware that he was an embarrassment to his father. He felt alienated from his family even though his mother felt sorry for him and babied him to boost his self-image. Throughout junior high and high school Jim became increasingly bitter, and conflicts in the family grew—conflicts that usually centered around him.

After graduation from high school, Jim was labeled the "black sheep" and rarely came around the family. When he did, old family dynamics took over, and the reunions were painful for everyone.

Was Jim the black sheep of the family? Was he the cause of their pain and embarrassment? Was his mother's babying responsible for Jim's failure to meet high academic standards? Or did the demands of an inflexible father exasperate Jim and prompt his rebellion? Who was really at fault, Jim or the family system?

Understanding the family as an interactive unit is crucial to understanding a child's behavior. Strong-willed children are easily alienated from the family system; they feel as if they don't belong or that their role is to be the "bad child." Their behavior, however, can be a helpful reflection on how the system is working. Observing and reflecting on the dynamics within the family can be the most beneficial approach to bringing needed changes for everyone involved.

Jesus, the Opposer

You may be shocked that your strong-willed child can actually play a positive role in healing your family. How could a "problem child" produce anything good? And yet, incredibly, Jesus himself played the role of the "opposer," confronting the pious, self-righteous religious leaders of his time. He saw through the facade of their religious acts and the sham of their outward appearances. His opposition was healthy and justified, but the religious authorities viewed it as rebellion. This was most evident when the institutionally religious disapproved of Jesus' associating with people they considered to be social outcasts. Jesus asked his listeners to make some critical judgments about who was "good" and who was "bad" as he related the parable of the two sons:

> What do you think? There was a man who had two sons. He went to the first and said, "Son, go and work today in the vineyard."
>
> "I will not," he answered, but later he changed his mind and went.
>
> Then the father went to the other son and said the same thing. He answered, "I will, sir," but he did not go.
>
> Which of the two did what his father wanted?
>
> "The first," they answered.
>
> Jesus said to them, "I tell you the truth, the tax collectors and the prostitutes are entering the kingdom of God ahead of you" (Matt. 21:28–31).

Jesus shattered the model of who was "good" and who was "bad." When the strong-willed child challenges our values, we need to be careful how we respond and what conclusions we make. Are we encountering disobedience that requires immediate correction, or the predictable response of a child who is reacting to rigidity or error in our parenting? If we do not understand the differences in our children and the motivation of their responses, we may simply fear their challenge, label them as "bad," and firmly entrench ourselves in cycles of conflict. When we react to their emotional outbursts and resistance, we play a part in an ongoing family power struggle.

How You Can Win and Still Lose

Power struggles in the home of a strong-willed child can take several forms. Remember what happened in the Townsend household at the opening of the chapter? Teddy behaved unreasonably ("If it's Monday, why does it feel like Saturday?. . .") and pushed his mother to the point of anger. Sarah saw only two options: She could either give in or explode in anger. If she gave in, she resented Teddy's power over her. If she exploded, she felt tremendous guilt, an experience prevalent in many Christian homes.

Parents who focus only on the child's behavior or who feel they must always maintain the position of power are quickly and easily hooked into escalating power struggles with a strong-willed child. When the child resists inflexible parenting through active defiance or passive rebellion, he may challenge deeply held parental values. Often parents fear that if they yield, they will lose the argument. They see their strength as being able to hold the line, but in actuality, it is also their weakness.

Power-oriented parents consistently confront the strong-willed child in order to force and demand submission. But their continual overreaction wounds the child's spirit instead of turning the child's will. Eventually the strong-willed child sees the selfishness of the parent who must win every battle. Over time a conscious or unconscious assessment is made that Mom or Dad simply cannot be trusted. Left unchecked, this attitude of distrust can create a lifetime of opposition to authority figures. The opposing child will tend to have more fights in life and will adopt a belief system that expects others to be unfair and unrewarding.

The opposite type of parents are afraid of conflict; they avoid it and pursue peace at any price. Their solution to the problem of a strong-willed child is to apply only kindness and love in an effort to coax the child's cooperation. Not only does this fail to win the child's long-term respect, but these parents find it difficult to establish daily boundaries in the home. Ultimately the child expects respect from everyone and demands support and kindness without having to earn it.

With dynamics like these, a parent can win the battle, but will most certainly lose the war. A strong-willed child hooked into conflict with either type of parent can destroy family harmony, and the resulting dynamics can damage the future psychological health of the child and, indeed, of everyone in the family.

Breaking the Cycle

This chapter began with a typical morning in the Townsend household. It may have ended with the conclusion that you, too, have a strong-willed child in your house—and you don't have a clue how to handle the situation. What you choose to do now is critical.

You can continue to distance yourself from your strong-willed child and wish the problem would go away. It won't. You can take an increasingly hard-line approach and hope that an iron hand will break the cycle of power struggles. It will fail.

Or you can take a new route. With the help of this book and the scriptural principles it contains, you can understand your strong-willed child or the child who is going through an oppositional phase. You can learn options for dealing with misbehavior other than strong-arm confrontations, bitter resignation, or running from conflict. You can discover biblical principles that will protect you and enable you to do a better job of parenting. Believe it or not, God can turn your unpleasant family relationships into more pleasant ones. You *can* have more success—and enjoyment—as a parent.

Most of all, you can experience firsthand how God's grace effectively applies to the relationships of parents and children. You can discover the only trustworthy basis for effective parenting: your relationship with a sovereign God who creates children, even strong-willed ones, so that we can learn from them.

Don't give up on becoming an effective parent. Don't give up on your child. In Christ, your home can yet be a trophy of his grace.

He is a home builder.

For Your Consideration

1. How do you feel about your relationship with your child? Are you angry? Do you blame yourself for your child's misbehavior? Do you feel defeated and powerless?

2. Consider your parenting style. Do you feel you must win every battle? Or do you strive for peace at any price? Or a mix of both?

3. What values do you hold that cause you the greatest amount of concern and fear when they are challenged by your children?

4. What roles do the children in your family play? Who is the compliant child? Who is the opposing child? Has this changed over time? How?

5. Do you blame someone in your family for the problems you face? Is it you or someone else? Can you change this blame into something constructive? How?

6. Is your discipline style causing more problems than it solves? What do you need to do to correct the situation?

Skill Builders

Emotionally Disengage. When your child opposes you, it's easy to respond emotionally with a fight-or-flight attitude. A fight response moves you into a combative encounter. A flight response moves you to surrender and withdraw. It's better to gain emotional neutrality than to argue from a gut-level emotional response. Here are some techniques to enable you to disengage emotionally:

1. What specific actions, words, or attitudes does your child use to hook you into emotional reactions? List them and commit them to God. Be honest with God about your feelings, and ask for his strength to keep you from reacting.

2. When you're in conflict with your child, pay attention to the feelings that you experience. Work at separating your thoughts from your feelings.

3. When you are angry with your child or anxious about the relationship, take a personal time-out. Work through your thoughts and emotions away from the source of conflict. Resolve your feelings without depending on your child's cooperation.

4. Don't view every resistance by your child as a personal affront. Resistance doesn't always have to be classified as rebellion. Make it an opportunity for dialogue.

Chapter Two

Caught in Conflict

Starting a quarrel is like breaching a dam;
so drop the matter before a dispute breaks out.
Proverbs 17:14

One of my early memories is sitting next to my father as he tried to teach me how to read. Unfortunately, dyslexia had not yet been identified, but it was doing its backward best in me. With the best of intentions he reviewed the page in front of me, but I could not read it correctly. I wasn't trying to frustrate my dad, but invariably my mistakes upset him, and he sternly demanded that I *think!* I felt stupid and afraid. I lost my ability to concentrate and panicked as I tried to pronounce the words—words that never matched what was on the page. The harder I tried, the more I failed and the more he exerted pressure on me, until mercifully the session ended. While he tried to help me succeed, deep down he wondered if I was stupid—and I wondered too.

Sometimes parents' failed attempts to do the right thing have more serious consequences. Franklin and Margaret were career missionaries. They were hard-working and faithful. Franklin died on the mission field, and Margaret raised her three daughters through adolescence into adulthood. Her desire was to see her daughters follow in their parents footsteps, serving Christ on their own mission fields. To insure that they did, she began to warn them at an early age to maintain their sexual purity. She not only taught and reminded them, but she nagged and hounded them as she monitored their behavior with a steely eye.

Now, twenty years later, Margaret sat in my study, a bitter, resentful woman. Each of her daughters had become sexually promiscuous in her teens and continued an immoral lifestyle into her thirties. Margaret was devastated.

"This has ruined our reputations," she said bitterly.

Margaret was convinced that each illicit act of sex by her daughters was a vengeful, deliberate effort to sabotage everything for which she and Franklin stood.

"How could they do this to us?" she asked.

But the daughters also had a story to tell, and they told it with anger and venom.

"Mom never trusted us," one of them said bitterly. "She made it very clear whenever we did something wrong. She criticized us for every mistake we made. It's all her fault we're the way we are!"

The more I listened, the more I realized that each of these women had received a steady dose of condemnation, angry warnings, and hostile tirades long before they gave their bodies away. Margaret was desperately afraid her daughters would be spiritual failures. She demanded sexual purity, but withheld acceptance and respect. By withholding acceptance until her demands were met, she expressed selfishness instead of love. One by one, each daughter descended into a promiscuous lifestyle, actually thinking that her mother owed *her* an apology and unrealistic acceptance. Each one overlooked Margaret's desire for her spiritual welfare and concluded that Margaret was legalistic and cold. Margaret and her daughters demanded specific responses from each other that both sides withheld. It was a tragic case of a parent's good intentions gone wrong.

What could my dyslexia and Margaret's daughters possibly have in common? More than you may imagine. In my case, my father's intentions were good and honorable. He wanted me to read well. Margaret wanted daughters who were pure, ready for the ministry she envisioned. But in both cases, a dynamic prevailed that produced the opposite result from that which was desired. I couldn't read and became afraid to try—it wasn't until I graduated from college that my skills improved. Margaret's daughters abandoned everything she believed in.

Proverbs 14:12 says, "There is a way that seems right to a man, but in the end it leads to death." What seems right from our perspective often produces deadly results. In parenting this may mean that what you want to achieve in your child is not at all what you end up producing.

Margaret and her daughters got caught in ongoing power struggles or, as I call them, "loops." Loops result from the emotional reaction of parents to the negative behavior of their child or from a child's emotional response to the behavior of the parents. In these reactive cycles, each person blames the other person's behavior or attitude for problems in the relationship. Consciously or unconsciously, their judgments perpetuate the conflict, because they prompt a continual cycle of emotional reactions.

A loop is an ongoing battle of the wills. Parents attempt to get the behavior they want from their strong-willed child but inevitably meet with opposition. The opposition may be active rebellion or passive resistance. Parents may desire a legitimate or godly goal, but if they express their desire emotionally, out of selfishness or fear, quarrels and arguments result.

Emotional Reactions and the Cycle of Loops

Power struggles result when a parent and a child desire two different things and react emotionally to each other. Be assured, every family falls into power struggles at various stages of family life. The danger occurs when occasional power struggles become loops. Once they begin, they are extremely difficult to break. Over time, loops create a hostile family atmosphere. A loop is not caused by one person, but

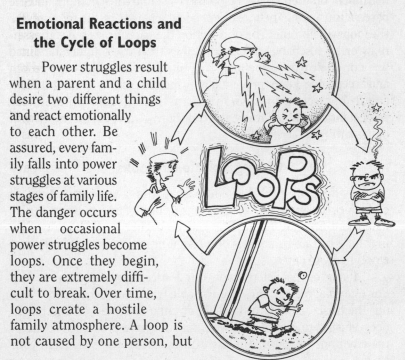

two people interacting in reactive ways that create a cycle that ends with both people feeling bad.

Loops usually revolve around a specific issue that becomes the "hot spot" between the parent and the strong-willed child. These issues result from the emotional reactions of the parent. For example, a mother may conclude that if her son does not quit associating with a certain friend in school, he will become a gang member. If a father sees behavior in his son that reminds him of his cousin who served prison time, he fears that his son will end up behind bars too. Hot spots may be simple issues of doing chores, doing homework, or talking on the phone.

These parents are telling themselves scary stories about their children that may not be realistic. When they act on these fearful emotions and make emotional demands to force behavior, a loop will develop. The fact that parents make demands indicates that they are dependent on their child's response. The child must comply, and the parents must win. The more dependent a parent is, the more severe the loop will become. The only option the parent may see is to withdraw or try to change the child, rather than try to understand and work on their part in the loop. The ultimate casualties are freedom and acceptance. Loops prevent family members from making choices and being accepted for who they are. Parents and children lose respect for each other. And most tragically, God's plan for the growth of the family is sacrificed.

Casting Emotional Hooks

By now you probably know what things your strong-willed child does or says to engage you in your part of a loop. But you may have more difficulty identifying how you begin a loop—how, in "fishing" for a certain response, you prompt or invite your child to react emotionally to you.

It may be that you present your desires in an inappropriate way. For example, maybe you were irritable when you demanded, "Take out the trash—and do it now!" Your child felt attacked and lashed out, refusing to do the task. You may not have even been aware of the emotions in you that invited this negative response from your child. Power struggles arise from seemingly insignificant encounters such as this.

Margaret, in the beginning of the chapter, desired sexual purity from her daughters. But she "fished" for their response with a hook baited with fear and suspicion. Margaret actually invited her daughters' resentment and rebellion; in their mother's fear the daughters saw mistrust and condemnation.

Ultimately, however, it's unimportant who starts a loop. As the adult, you need to be aware that a loop is occurring and to accept responsibility for your part in it. You also need to know how to refuse to participate, even if you were the one who started the loop. Because emotions fuel the dynamics of a loop, understanding its emotional component is the place to begin, especially if you have a strong-willed child.

Loops are at their worst when the mood is tense. When you're tired, angry, threatened, grieving, pressured, or emotionally needy, you're susceptible to inviting a loop or being hooked into one. Strong-willed children typically have a low tolerance for discomfort and inconvenience, and when they complain, they can be the target of other family members. And once a loop begins, it seems to have a life of its own. The Lopez family is a realistic example.

On a cross-country car trip, the needle on the enthusiasm gauge was pointing dangerously toward empty. While everyone was tired of freeway views and counting license plates, nine-year-old Maria held nothing back.

"When are we going to get to the motel?"

"I want to get out!"

"Make James quit touching me!"

Her mother's patience, already a bit stretched, began to wear down.

"Give it a rest, Maria," she said. "We're all tired and hungry. You're starting to make everybody miserable with your complaining!"

The other kids were doing their part to hang in there, her mother thought. If Maria could just be a little more accepting of inconvenience, the final miles would go quickly.

"What a vacation!" Maria snapped. "I'd rather be in school than stuck in this stupid car!"

"And that's just where I wish you were!" her mom said sarcastically. "Sometimes you're a bigger baby than your two-year-old sister. Just be quiet and give us all some peace!"

The freeway may have been asphalt, but Mr. Lopez was driving on eggshells. Maria and her mother continued to vent frustration on each other and everybody in the car. While Dad gripped the wheel, the other Lopez children secretly wished he would put Mom and Maria in the trunk.

A strong-willed child like Maria provides more than enough invitations to which you can react. She may withhold something you want. She may defy and challenge you. She may make tyrannical demands for things or constantly ignore your limits. She may feel that life's rules don't apply to her and find herself in constant trouble. Or she may be so emotionally volatile that you are drawn with magnetic force into loops you find difficult to resist.

You may think you need to endure loops with your strong-willed child, but they are detrimental to your relationship. These reactive loops create roles that are unhealthy when taken to the extreme. When a loop reaches its breaking point, parents feel like destroying the child or sending him away. As one mother told me in exasperation, "I just wish I could divorce my teenager."

Learning to Cut the Line

The opposing child who does not learn to cooperate or yield will find life difficult. If your only strategy is to challenge a strong-willed child, you may actually strengthen his resolve to resist you. This does not mean that the child should have his way. To be an effective parent you must take leadership but also avoid reacting emotionally and getting hooked into a loop. There are many strategies for diffusing emotional situations, but all do the same thing: they "cut the line" that is hooking you and your child in a loop.

In unhealthy families, desires and feelings control relationships, making loops unavoidable. The answer, however, is not to suppress emotions, but to deal with them biblically. In Psalm 139:23–24, David asks God, "Search me, O God, and know my heart; test me and know my anxious thoughts. See if there is any offensive way in me, and lead me in the way everlasting." God does not condemn us for our emotions, but he does call us to be aware of them, to confess them, and to submit them to the working of the Holy Spirit. When we are in conflict with our strong-willed child, our response should be like David's: to bring our whole lives, emotions included, to God and ask him to lead us into loving, respectful relationships.

Kathryn was in counseling because of a strained relationship with her eight-year-old son, Marty. She had learned to be aware of her part in their loops and what to do in response to Marty's attitudes and behaviors. But whenever she was tired or irritable, Marty challenged her with greater anger and defiance, and she responded in kind.

"It's like he has an antenna," she said. "He detects my weak and vulnerable moments and makes them harder for me."

Through counseling Kathryn began to see that Marty was actually a sensitive child, keenly able to detect tension in the family. When he perceived it, he vented his own emotions in order to find release. Kathryn viewed this behavior as insensitivity to others. She wanted him to ignore tensions, or at least minimize them the way she did. For Marty, however, a good fight cleared the air. The same couldn't be said for Kathryn, who vowed not to get hooked into an argument again.

One Saturday in January, Kathryn had an unusually tough day. She was involved in a fender-bender that led to a fight with her husband, Rick. On the heels of the accident her mother called and unloaded her post-holiday frustration.

"Kathryn, next year I'll expect you and the family to be at my house first thing Christmas morning," she scolded. "I can't tell you how disappointed I was that you didn't come over until late in the afternoon. I don't appreciate being in second place!"

Kathryn did her best to explain that Rick's parents deserved a chance to be with the children on Christmas morning, but it was no use. Kathryn's mother was wrapping this post-Christmas present in guilt and a big black bow. Kathryn could feel herself sinking emotionally as she hung up and handed Marty his lunch.

"I hate this junk!" Marty whined. "Why can't you make good stuff like Jeremy's mom?"

Kathryn spun to see Marty slouching in his chair, scowling alternately at the sandwich and her. She could feel her emotions rising but she didn't want to fight. She didn't want to get hooked again.

"Marty," she said deliberately, "I've really had a tough morning. Please don't make it any more difficult."

"What did I do?" Marty snapped. "I get blamed for everything!"

Kathryn was hooked. She had tried to be kind but Marty traded evil in exchange for her good.

"All you think about is yourself, and believe me, I'm sick of you!" she yelled. "Go to your room!"

Marty mumbled something indistinguishable under his breath and stomped off. Kathryn had done it again; she was emotionally drained, and Marty had drawn her in. She needed time to sort things out and pray.

"Lord, help me to be full of you and not react to Marty," she asked.

After a cooling-off period, she headed to Marty's room.

"Marty, do you feel like I attacked you without reason?" she asked as she sat on the edge of Marty's bed.

Marty looked stunned by the gentleness of her question.

"You blame me for everything," he repeated irritably.

This time Kathryn saw the invitation and sidestepped it.

"That's because absolutely everything in life *is* your fault," she teased, a smile spreading across her face.

Marty tried to hang on to his bad mood but grinned in spite of himself.

"Well, but I don't like it when you yell at me," he explained.

"And I don't like it when you whine and gripe about the meals I fix you," Kathryn responded gently. "Can you think of another way you could have asked for a different lunch?"

Kathryn and Marty continued to talk about responding with kindness. Kathryn knew Marty wouldn't be a changed kid, but at least this particular incident had a happy ending. Even though Marty hooked Kathryn when she was down, she "cut the line" and successfully avoided a second argument. What's more, she built a communications bridge that changed their relationship for the rest of the day.

Types of Reactionary Loops

There are many different kinds of reactionary loops in family life, but they all have one thing in common: they force the participants to react against each other so strongly that they become locked into polarized roles. That's why you may see rational parents with emotional children, hard-working parents with lazy children, aggressive parents with passive children, and so on. The intensity of the loop cements the roles between parent and child until the contrasts are dramatic: Moral–immoral, smart–dumb, social–anti-social, good–bad, optimistic–pessimistic, competent–incompetent, spiritual–worldly. Almost any belief or behavior can become an issue that fuels a loop and forces people into reactive roles.

Your ability to recognize loops will make it easier to avoid them. As you examine the most common loops that follow, pray that God will open your eyes so that your family will learn to care for each other and God's healing may begin.

Demander-Withholder

The most basic power struggle is the Demander-Withholder loop. In this dynamic, one person makes demands while the other withholds what is desired. The frustrated Demander increases the pressure to the point of becoming domineering, invasive, critical, or angry. The Demander believes that increasing demands until the Withholder yields is the only solution available. Winning is everything. Conversely, the Withholder believes that the only solution possible is to fearfully withdraw or angrily withhold in order to gain a measure of protection.

Ironically, neither person may be conscious of the strategy being employed, and so the loop intensifies. Usually the parent and child feel victimized by the loop and wish the other person would behave differently. The Withholder wishes the Demander would quit being so domineering, and the Demander wishes the Withholder would be less passive and more responsive. As the loop intensifies they lose trust and respect for each other until goodwill and cooperation vanish—just as they did in Gary's house.

Gary's father was livid. Gary had lied to him again.

As the counseling session began, Gary and his father, Dennis, both shifted uneasily in their chairs. Dennis broke the silence.

"I guess Gary is going to be a liar all his life. He told me he'd been turning in his homework, but he lied," he said, casting an accusing glance at Gary.

Gary's head was bowed. He was clearly angry at his father's attitude but refused to respond.

"What happens when you don't tell your father the truth?" I asked Gary.

"He gets mad and yells at me," Gary said quickly.

"Then what?"

"Then I feel bad and don't want to talk to him."

"What happens when you don't talk to him?"

"I don't know," Gary said with a rising resentment. "Why don't you ask him?"

"Okay, Dad, what happens?" I asked.

"I feel like he's trying to hide something from me and it makes me nervous," Dennis responded.

"So what do you do then?"

"Well, I get angry and demand that he talk to me," he said. "But he just gets up and goes off to his room."

This was a Demander-Withholder loop in full swing: Gary's dad demanded communication and Gary withdrew.

I asked Dennis if he could back off and ease the pressure he exerted on Gary.

"If Gary would tell the truth, I wouldn't have to be so demanding," he said.

I asked Gary if he could be more open and honest.

"Well—if Dad won't be so angry, I will," he said.

Up to this point, Gary and his father had a major investment in changing each other's behavior. Each was so dependent on the other's response that they weren't able to see the loop in which they were trapped and how each one kept it going. Gary wouldn't be truthful without a guarantee of safety, and his father wouldn't ease the pressure until he heard the truth. Gary and his father needed to deal with their roles in the loop regardless of the other's actions. By taking personal responsibility for words and behaviors, the relationship could begin to heal.

Pursuer-Distancer

A second common power struggle is the Pursuer-Distancer loop. This loop is common during the teenage years when parents feel their teen becoming distant. They feel insecure as their child moves her loyalties from them to friends or to herself. With new loyalties, the teen may become opposing and distant, inviting the parent to pursue her if they want to have a relationship.

Parents pursue in many ways. They ask questions, sometimes going to the extreme of playing the FBI. Some make extra efforts to contribute to the relationship or make conscious sacrifices to prove their sincerity. Others lecture, hoping to coerce cooperation. Strong-willed teens interpret these and other behaviors as engulfing and smothering them. Their gut-level response is to distance themselves and resist communication, grunting answers or hiding behind a disinterested "I don't know."

Teenagers who are being pursued feel swallowed up and they distance themselves as a natural defense. "It's my life," the strong-willed teen declares, as if that should earn the desired independence. Some teens isolate themselves and become secretive. Their body language screams, "I'm not going to let you in!" They won't look you in the eye. They cross their arms, turn their head, and sigh resentfully. I've even seen them cover their eyes or ears during conversations! No wonder parents are frustrated. But they continue to pursue their withdrawing teen to the point of being disrespectful. This only strengthens the Pursuer-Distancer loop.

The Pursuer-Distancer loop feeds off a simple dynamic: the teenager asserts independence and creates distance, while the parents pursue, smothering the teen. This loop, like all others, produces alienation followed by separation. It's especially discouraging because of the separation that is a natural part of the teenage years. During this period, teens normally seek their own identities instead of being extensions of parents and their value systems.

If parents can step back and disengage from the Pursuer-Distancer loop, they can initiate healing. To do so, they will need to trust

God in their teen's life. Conversely, if the teenager will be respectful and earn freedoms instead of demand them, parents will find it easier to relax. This enables them to grant the freedom teens need to develop the independence and competence to become healthy, godly adults. When parents and teenagers are locked into the Pursuer-Distancer loop, they often need help from a pastor, counselor, or support group. Lucy knows this well.

Lucy was a kind and loving mom who was highly involved with each of her children. When her normally loving daughter Sarah reached fourteen, she "went off the deep end," as Lucy said. Sarah became secretive about her activities and began to distance herself from her mother. Not only was Lucy hurt, but she panicked when Sarah didn't respond to her. To span the gulf, Lucy pursued Sarah but was met with indifference. Lucy felt rejected and resented Sarah's cold, aloof attitudes. But Lucy was undaunted. Every day when Sarah came home from school Lucy greeted her, asked her how her day went, and sought out conversation. Invariably Sarah acted as if this was a great imposition. Lucy took the rejection for a while, but soon her exasperation boiled over.

"I'm just being friendly, and this is the way you treat me? And after all the things I've done for you!"

Lucy brought her daughter to counseling, and I asked Sarah how she felt being around her mother.

"Bad! I feel guilty and just plain bad," she said.

Lucy was offended and moved to her own defense.

"That's because you treat *me* so bad," she charged.

Both sat in silence for a moment. As we discussed their relationship, they realized how they were impacting each other. Along with a few tears, the apologies began to flow. While confession alone won't break a loop, it is a starting place. Lucy and Sarah acknowledged their roles in the loop and asked forgiveness of each other.

Lucy needed to become more of a follower and less of a pursuer. In application this meant that she needed to avoid barraging Sarah with questions and look for more subtle openings to initiate conversation. Sarah needed to learn how to be an initiator of conversation with her mother. For her, application meant working on simple courtesies like saying "hi" when she entered the house. With repentance that expressed itself in practical applications, Sarah and Lucy discovered more flexibility in their relationship and broke free of the mold that the Pursuer-Distancer loop was imposing on them.

Controller-Rebel

This loop is common with parents of strong-willed children. A parent bent on controlling a child invites rebellious behavior, or a rebellious child invites a parent to be controlling. A Controller-Rebel loop forms until parents and children find themselves stuck in rigid roles with destructive consequences.

Margaret and her daughters, at the beginning of the chapter, are a perfect example. Margaret was bent on keeping her daughters sexually pure. She attempted to control their behavior—behavior they hadn't even exhibited yet—through lecturing and demanding. Her daughters rebelled against the pressure by doing precisely what Margaret forbade them to do.

A child who is strong-willed from Day One can easily invite his parents into a Controller-Rebel loop. Jack and Nancy were an easygoing couple until their son Michael came along. Before he was even a year old, Michael became adept at voicing his opinions. His first words, predictably, were "No way!" Both Jack and Nancy realized that life would soon be utter chaos if they didn't nip Michael's behavior in the bud. So they instituted what they thought was a logical and reasonable system of rewards, punishments, and behavioral expectations, complete with sticker charts and a time-out chair. But Michael would have none of it. The sticker chart went in the toilet and the time-out chair down the basement steps. The more Michael rebelled, the more Jack and Nancy tried to enforce their behavioral system. By the time Michael was three years old, the family was deeply entrenched in a Controller-Rebel loop.

Rescuer-Victim

If a child feels continually helpless or inadequate and acts on these feelings, a parent may feel compelled to rescue the child, and eventually a Rescuer-Victim loop is created. Every child experiences times of self-doubt and nervousness about his abilities. But if a child is chronically helpless, or if his parents respond in unhealthy ways, a loop may develop that will reinforce the child's inadequacy.

This loop can be seen in many families during homework sessions. What parents haven't heard, "I don't understand this assignment" or "I can't do this—it's too hard"? Some parents sympathize too deeply with the child, try to help him, and end up doing the homework for him. The child learns that he really can't do the work, and Mom or Dad must help him.

Other parents refuse to help. "You're a fourth-grader now. You don't need any help. All the other kids in your class are doing the same assignment." At this point the child may feel abandoned. He whines, rages, or gives up on the homework. If the parents feel guilty for not helping or can't deal with his frustration, they may end up doing the child's assignment for him anyway.

In either case, the child's helpless behavior draws the parents into rescuing him, and the parents' intervention reinforces the child's helplessness and irresponsibility. Because strong-willed children have a tendency to avoid responsibility, Rescuer-Victim loops are common in their families. This loop is also prevalent in families where a child has a learning disorder, a physical disability, is hyperactive, or has an attention deficit disorder. While this loop develops from good intentions, it will become harmful if it is not abandoned.

Husband-Wife

Even though we are focusing on the relationships between parents and children, there's one major loop that is easily overlooked: it's the parental loop, most often characterized by a good guy-bad guy polarization. Parents are to work as teammates, expressing mutual trust and respect in the task of parenting.

In the Husband-Wife loop, however, one parent gives the child permission to oppose while the other parent attempts to discipline. The child receives mixed messages, and the parental alliance is weakened.

A Husband-Wife loop can happen when a father who assumes the traditional role of disciplinarian disciplines excessively out of anger. This invites the wife to defend the child out of her traditional role of nurturer. If she becomes too closely aligned with the child, the father feels frustrated and sees the wife as undermining his authority. A loop is created when he vents this frustration on the child and his wife comes to the rescue again. If the husband and wife have difficulty discussing the loop, the problem will escalate. Karl and Becky are examples of parents caught in this loop.

HUSBAND-WIFE LOOP

DAD ATTACKS SON

MOM ALLIES WITH KIDS

DAD GETS LEFT OUT

After a hard day at work, Karl had little patience with the noise and confusion that swirled through the Kramer house as they prepared for dinner. The bickering and arguing about whose turn it was to set the table, who sat next to Dad, and who should unload the dishwasher brought out the worst in Karl. After several requests for the boys to settle down and get their jobs done, Karl would snap and spew rude and abusive comments so the boys would see that he was serious. But Becky was serious, too. She didn't appreciate her children being used as verbal punching bags for Karl's frustration, and she wasted no time in coming to their defense.

"Becky, you're so permissive that these boys will never learn how to be responsible!" he charged.

"I'm not as concerned about their responsibility as I am your language! You're crushing these kids!" Becky fired back.

And taking it all in were the boys, especially Josh. He was already closer to his mother than to his father, and he was having trouble submitting to the authority of teachers in school. Earlier in the week he brought home a pink slip for sassing a teacher, and now he watched as his parents exchanged heated words. His mother's unknowing defense was all he needed to get in a few shots of his own.

"Come on, Dad!" he snapped. "You're always dissin' us!"

Karl scowled but said nothing. Without Becky's support and with Josh's challenge, he was outnumbered.

Later that night Karl and Becky rehashed the confrontation. Karl explained how he felt about always being the "bad guy," while Becky confessed she found it hard not to protect her sons when she saw Karl verbally attacking them.

Karl was angry at Becky because of the alienation he sensed. He actually felt like chucking it all and living by himself. Over the next few days Karl struggled with his feelings of being an outsider and wondered how he could change Becky's behavior in siding with the boys. Becky was mired in her struggles too. She wanted to change Karl and his dynamics with the boys. She wanted him to put more emphasis on his relationship with them and wondered how she could bring it about. She also pondered how they could diffuse their conflicts. She had a thought, and it proved to be the key in leading them out of the Good Guy-Bad Guy loop. She shared it with Karl a few nights later.

"We need a signal," she said. "Something we can use to slow these situations down and avoid division in front of the kids."

Karl was embarrassed that his weakness demanded special attention, but he knew Becky was right.

"Let's do this," he said. "When my mouth gets ahead of common sense, why don't you take off your glasses and rub your eyes as if they're tired. The kids won't really notice, but I'll know that we need to get away and talk."

Through practice, perseverance, and the work of the Holy Spirit, Karl's and Becky's signal followed by discussion presented a united front. Prior to their discovery, each one reacted to the other's behavior and produced a response that was exactly opposite to what the other partner wanted. Now Karl and Becky demonstrated mutual respect by listening to each other, which allowed them to be on the same team in their parenting. Karl began weeding out disrespectful speech and concentrated on relating with the boys. Becky began to see that love also meant being tough. She worked on enabling her sons to emotionally wean from her and become more responsible.

The complexity of this loop is compounded in today's culture where husband-wife roles in discipline and nurture are sometimes reversed. A stay-at-home mother whose responsibilities include all of the organizing, disciplining, training, and maintenance of the household may resent it when her husband comes home from his job each night and spends the evening relaxing and playing with the children. She is the Bad Guy who must maintain order and keep track of the long-term plans, while he is the Good Guy who is spontaneous and playful.

By focusing on their own behaviors, however, husbands and wives can break free of loops and become better parents and better spouses. They can eventually learn to value each other as parents and create an alliance that prompts healthy parenting, free of the Good Guy-Bad Guy loop.

Changing Reactive Loops

It can be done. Amid all the complexities and emotion of reactive loops, you can still break free of them. You've already seen the first steps:

- Identify the loop in which you are trapped.
- Look for the emotions that drive it.
- Know your part in the loop. Take a critical view of your words and actions that invite the loop.
- Make the commitment to sidestep the invitations to a loop that comes your way.

All of these are first steps toward freedom and relationship. But there are two final principles to consider.

First, you need to accept the dynamics of your family life as they are. Relax, quit fighting and reacting to the way things are. When you do this, you're acknowledging your family's reality rather than wishing things were different. Doing that is an acknowledgment that God is sovereign—not just in principle, but also in your home. When you let go of the responsibility to change your child's behavior single-handedly, you're acknowledging God's role in his or her life. You're free to be less demanding and more responsive. Relationship can take priority over power. That in itself brings positive changes in relating with your child. Believing that God is in charge produces an inner strength that fosters emotional neutrality. You don't have to react to your child.

Second, even with all you've learned about loops, realize that knowledge alone is not enough. Personal growth and personal change on your part is mandatory. Make no mistake, breaking loops in your family relationships comes down to you and your choices. Maybe the loops in which you're trapped are ones in which your parents struggled. Loops can easily endure for generations unless parents take personal responsibility for them and break the family pattern. But what motivates choices and growth like this?

Jesus is the ultimate motivator in breaking family loops and creating new patterns. Don't expect your family to be motivated to change or reward you for your efforts. If they're part of the loop, they may not recognize the problem. In fact, they may even persecute you for initiating godly relationships and healthy patterns.

If you are too focused on family members' responses or dependent on them to initiate change, you can easily lose your motivation for doing your part. Changing yourself and your patterns of relating is difficult, but focusing on Christ rather than results will lift you above feelings and circumstances. Support groups are invaluable for this and may supply the tangible encouragement you need to follow God and work free of the entanglement of reactive loops.

If you're breaking loops and bringing change in your family, you are ministering God's love and righteousness. Think ahead to what awaits you, even beyond restored family relationships. Think ahead to seeing Christ face-to-face and hearing for yourself, "Well done, good and faithful servant!"

For Your Consideration

1. What family situations or issues invite you into loops with your children?
2. How do you typically react when under stress? In what ways does your strong-willed child aggravate these reactions?
3. Which loop identified in this chapter is most commonly experienced between you and your strong-willed child?

(Demander-Withholder, Pursuer-Distancer, Victim-Rescuer, etc.) Do you seem to have a loop that doesn't correspond with those discussed in this chapter? What words characterize the loop?

4. What are the negative consequences of loops in your family?

5. What are the strongest emotions you feel when you are in a loop? In what ways do you act on these emotions?

6. Think back to the most recent conflict with your strong-willed child. Did you hook your child into a conflict or did he hook you? What did each of you do to keep the conflict going? Is this conflict part of an ongoing loop?

7. What solutions are you currently using in your difficulties with your child that do not solve the problems or make them worse?

8. Does your relationship with your spouse create or diminish loops with your child?

9. How can God help you disengage from loops?

Skill Builders

Reflective Listening. Loops occur from emotional pain in relationships. But they can be broken over time through emotional and spiritual maturity. As people mature in healthy environments, they learn to express their feelings honestly, respectfully, and effectively. Effective expression, however, is not enough; we must learn to listen effectively as well.

Reflective listening is a skill that enables you to be responsive instead of reactive. It is respectful listening, and can replace reactive loops found in families that listen poorly and do not validate each other's worth. It is one of the most valuable skills a parent can have. "Everyone should be quick to listen, slow to speak and slow to become angry, for man's anger does not bring about the righteous life God desires" (James 1:19–20).

Reflective listening is developed by summarizing, paraphrasing, and acknowledging what a person is thinking, feeling, and desiring. When it is successfully employed, it can help you sidestep a loop by disengaging emotionally. Here is a sample dialogue that illustrates how reflective listening is used:

Child: "You always take Johnny's side!" *(An attack and invitation to defend yourself)*

Parent: "It sounds like you're angry with me and that you don't think I care about how you feel." *(Parent reflects back the feelings of the child)*

Child: "Yeah! If you cared about me, you wouldn't be so unfair. Johnny never gets in trouble!"

Parent: "Johnny didn't fail his class. *(Honest statement)* You're being disciplined as a consequence of your behavior, and what you're telling me is that you think that's unfair." *(Reflection of child's thoughts)*

Child: "Well . . . I'm angry—and I'm tired of not doing well in school." *(Said with more softness in his voice)*

Parent: "Son, I know it's hard when we don't succeed. It's easy to get upset." *(Parent reflects and treats son's reactions as normal)*

Child: "Dad, I'm discouraged. And I don't think more study time and less TV will make any difference."

Parent: "Well, work doesn't always pay off the way we expect, and that is discouraging. But I believe that it's one of the ways that you learn and grow." *(Reflection of feelings and honest statements)*

Child: "So I have to give up some TV time and study more?"

Parent: "Yes, Son, you do."

Chapter Three

Building Parental Authority

He who spares the rod hates his son,
but he who loves him is careful to discipline him.

Proverbs 13:24

Mark is a total tyrant," Lisa said. "We can't do anything without his fighting it."

Lisa and her husband Wayne sat in my office, relating the problems they were having with their five-year-old son, Mark. This was a couple in defeat, on the verge of emotional bankruptcy. It wasn't as if they hadn't tried. They'd attempted to coerce Mark into obedience, but the fallout wasn't worth it.

RE-ESTABLISHING PARENTAL AUTHORITY

"We've tried to force him to obey, but his attitude makes us completely miserable," Lisa said, glancing at Wayne who nodded in agreement.

"We've decided that we just can't go anywhere with him, so most of the time we just stay home," Wayne added.

After listening to the litany of his behavior, I realized Mark's parents were actually intimidated by their son. Not only was Mark bright, but he was manipulative and cruel.

"I'm gonna kill you and cut you into little pieces and enjoy it 'cuz I hate you," he once told his mom.

The threat served its purpose. Lisa was afraid of Mark, and she dealt with him cautiously and with reservation. She wasn't in charge, and Wayne wasn't much help either. He simply tried to ignore the magnitude of Mark's defiance.

Wayne and Lisa weren't building parental authority. When Lisa tried to exert authority, she vacillated between two extremes. If she took Mark on toe-to-toe, the encounter ended in an explosion and a fight. That made her feel guilty, so she swung to the other extreme, failing to set limits and withdrawing from Mark because she didn't enjoy being around him. Withdrawal left Lisa feeling powerless and inadequate as a mother. And none of this was lost on Mark, who developed his own mindset as a result of ineffective parenting. In his eyes, life's rules did not apply to him. He was exempt from anybody's authority, or so he thought. Life was his to shape as he saw fit.

As strange as it may seem, many parents feel very vulnerable around their children. They haven't established protection for themselves or their children in the form of effective limits on behavior and verbal or emotional expression. As a result, their families aren't safe places, especially in an emotional sense. Without authority and protective limits, hurt, fear, and anger are continually experienced by family members.

While human authority can be misused, godly authority establishes order so that families experience safety in their relationships. Potent, competent parenting keeps loops to a minimum and diminishes their consequences. While all children need limits, strong-willed children have a special need for authority to help them understand the limits of their own personal power.

Parenting takes skill, and for Lisa and Wayne, competency was going to require hard work and diligence. Mark wasn't going to be remade in an evening—he said so himself.

I asked Wayne and Lisa to bring Mark in so that I could meet with the family. It didn't take long for Mark to signal his intent.

"If you think you can make me behave, you're wrong," he said defiantly.

"Would you like me to try?" I asked.

"I'll call Child Protective Services if you do," he shot back.

This was one sharp kid!

"Actually, Mark, I want to teach your parents how to help you behave."

Mark's eyes narrowed, measuring the seriousness of the threat before him.

"They'll never be able to do it," he said calmly.

"So would you like to see if they can?" I asked respectfully.

Mark's reply was a simple, non-emotional, "Yes."

In the sessions that followed, I encouraged Lisa and Wayne to take their parenting seriously. Though they were ready to accept their responsibility to be parents, without authority they were powerless. They needed to establish limits to protect Mark from his selfish behavior. If they didn't, somebody later in life would—somebody like a federal prison. They needed a game plan and mutual support to establish tough love and parental authority.

Mark needed an object lesson about who was in charge. He needed to see that his parents deserved and required his cooperation and obedience. Up to now, their words meant nothing. Mark required a significant object lesson in order to relocate the center of authority in his life. Lisa and Wayne had to get on top of their problem—literally. They listened to my plan, swallowed deeply, and agreed to implement it.

"Mark," his father said a few days later when Mark was being especially challenging, "I think you've lost sight of who's in charge around here."

With that, Wayne safely but deliberately wrestled Mark to the carpet and sat on him. For the next hour, father and son maintained that posture, much to Mark's fierce opposition. He spat, kicked and even cursed at his father, but Wayne was immovable.

"Okay! I'll be good!" he yelled.

"I've heard that before," Wayne said. "I need to know that I can trust you."

Mark was incensed and tried to bite Wayne on the leg, but he only managed to get a mouthful of sweat pants. After Wayne's shift was done, Lisa took her turn, assuming the position vacated by her husband. Mark went ballistic. Again he fought, cried, screamed, and cursed. And though Wayne and Lisa found this physically and emotionally exhausting, they supported each other and held their ground. Wayne and Lisa were over a hundred pounds heavier than Mark and were physically capable of being more powerful than he was. Little by little, Mark's anger and rebellion subsided. When his endurance to fight was finally gone, his will followed suit.

"That's enough, Mommy," he whimpered. "I'll obey!"

It was a different Mark and a different atmosphere during the next counseling session. Wayne and Lisa said that they learned how critical it was not to give in until Mark demonstrated ownership for appropriate behavior. Even Mark agreed that he was learning. "But I didn't like being sat on!" he said.

It was obvious from Mark's demeanor that he had learned who was in charge. The peace in the family was remarkable, so much so that Lisa wondered if it could last.

Authority Through Respect

Most interventions—measures taken to change behavior—don't require actions as extreme as those employed by Wayne and Lisa. The key to building a safe family environment is to establish authority and to hold the line when it's challenged. This provides the structure, order, and limits on behavior that children need. If parents back away from exercising authority, they'll simply reinforce the inappropriate power a child wields in the family.

Your role as a parent is ordained by God. Even if you don't feel competent as a mother or father, your office has been established in heaven. This truth is extremely practical. When you know that you are serving God, you can avoid the trap of being dependent on your child's response to validate your authority. If you're looking for your child's applause to establish your role as parent, you'll have a long wait. You'll also be ineffective in the interim. But you can steadily earn respect as a parent through diligence and respectful treatment of your children.

There's no better way to earn respect than to give it yourself. Listen to your children. Consider thoughts and feelings as you make age-appropriate decisions with them or for them. And while you require and earn respect for yourself, insist that your children respect others too. Be reasonable and flexible, but above all, don't shrink away from the hard work of parenting.

This will mean confrontations and setting limits on their behavior. Proverbs 28:23 says "He who rebukes a man will in the end gain more favor than he who has a flattering tongue." Confronting your child and setting limits is hard work, but it's part of your biblical role, especially if you have a strong-willed child like Mark.

If setting limits and creating order is an area of weakness for you, a parent support group or help from a counselor may be beneficial. But every parent should ask several crucial questions: "Is my family emotionally safe?" "Do my children exercise power inappropriately?" "Do I need help to take charge of my family?"

You Must Intervene

Once you've assumed authority in your family, you have the right and responsibility to be treated accordingly. From that point on, squinting eyes and a defiant voice that proclaims "You're not my boss!" is a challenge that demands a response. This strong-willed child is inviting you to enter a loop in order to maintain self-centered behavior. While such a challenge will raise your emotional temperature, an authoritative but respectful response is required.

Sharon and Jim were struggling with Ericka, Sharon's fourteen-year-old daughter. Jim adopted Ericka after his marriage to Sharon, and he actually had a better relationship with her than her mother did. Ericka was moody and strong-willed, and so was Sharon.

Ericka's opposition to her parents was growing steadily. If Sharon and Jim made the slightest request, she fought them or, at the very least, obeyed with a chilly, put-upon attitude. This quickly drew Sharon into a loop in which mother and daughter ended up alienated from each other. But these skirmishes were nothing compared to the war that erupted at the pool.

Ericka was a competitive swimmer. At one particular meet, Sharon and Ericka began to argue over a trivial matter. A routine disagreement escalated until they became the main poolside event.

"Be quiet!" Sharon hissed. "You're making a fool of yourself!"

"I don't care!" Ericka shouted. "And I'm not yelling!"

Sharon needed to exert authority, but she was too emotionally entangled.

"Everyone is looking at us!" Sharon said angrily.

"Oh, Mother, nobody's looking at us! You're so paranoid!"

Sharon could not disengage.

"That's it! I'm withdrawing you from the meet!"

With that she turned toward the registration table to carry out her threat. Ericka couldn't believe her mother would do something so drastic.

"You can't do that!" she yelled, jumping down from the ledge where she was sitting. She reached for her mother in an attempt to stop her. By now, Sharon was an emotional powder keg. When she felt the hand on her arm, she pivoted and slapped her daughter hard on the side of the head, just as Jim entered the gate. Sharon ran to him and tried to explain the disaster that had just occurred.

Jim moved toward Ericka, and as he got within earshot, she began to curse at him. Ericka had never acted this way before. Jim took charge.

"Come on, Ericka, we're going home," he said firmly.

"You're not my father!" shouted Ericka.

Jim stood his ground and dodged another invitation to a loop. Inwardly he was seething at Ericka's insolence and venom, but he asserted his authority without reacting emotionally.

"I am your father, Ericka, and you'll get in the car or I'll carry you over to it," he said with convincing determination.

Ericka switched tactics, assuming the role of victim.

"Mom was yelling at me in front of my friends! And you saw what she did!"

"I know you're angry and upset with your mom," Jim said, "but you're still going to cooperate."

"I hate you! I hate both of you!" Ericka exploded.

"Get in the car," Jim said as he moved toward her.

Ericka knew her father was serious. Although she was furious, she wasn't going to risk being carried away in the arms of her father. She pushed past Jim and ran to the car, crying all the way. Nobody said a word on the trip home.

Despite the public embarrassment and emotional fireworks, Jim successfully intervened in several ways. First, he maintained a parental alliance with his wife, despite Sharon's failings. Second, he dodged each invitation to become hooked in a loop and calmly but firmly insisted on Ericka's cooperation. And finally, Jim didn't back down, even as the situation intensified in a public setting. When Ericka understood that Jim would dispassionately carry out his promise, she withdrew from the conflict.

When the family came for counseling the following week, Ericka's attitude had changed. There was a new softness about her. She was pleasant and cooperative. Even though the event at the pool hadn't brought about instant and complete change, Jim's correct use of authority taught Ericka that she could not win through arguments or tantrums.

Parents cannot force their child to change. What they can do is firmly but respectfully stand their ground and avoid the child's invitations to a loop. When the child realizes that he cannot win, he's more likely to assume his proper position in the family. This is no small challenge for parents. At times they may need to ignore their child's role and focus completely on their responsibilities as parents.

Many parents are wonderful at soft love. They are warm, accepting, responsive, and giving in their relationships with their children. But they do not initiate discipline. Because they're passive when it comes to requiring respect and obedience, their strength becomes their weakness. They're so sensitive to their children's feelings, they cannot weather the discomfort that comes with confrontation. These parents hope their sensitivity and kindness will cause their children to act the same way. But the strong-willed child doesn't know how to act this way and doesn't necessarily want to learn. This places "soft love" parents in a very vulnerable position.

Parents are to use authority to create order, place restraints, and make the home safe for every family member. This means they'll need to endure the disapproval of their child in the short term if they want their respect in the future.

Interventions do not magically change a child's behavior, but they are an important part of the learning process. Often one intervention is not enough, especially if the child is extremely strong-willed. It's easy for parents to become discouraged and avoid the hard work associated with having authority. Once they retreat, they become passive when circumstances are peaceful, but overreact when they are pushed beyond their limits. Intervening takes courage and diligence. And though interventions can be unpleasant and taxing, they pay big dividends. Can you afford to wait any longer?

Pick Your Battles Wisely

At this point, it may seem as if all you have to do to build authority is "draw the line" wherever and whenever you want. A wiser approach is to be strategic in your thinking, consciously and carefully picking your battles. Not everything is worth a conflict. Pick a battle that you can win. And make sure the victory is worth the price you will pay for it.

If you constantly find yourself in conflicts you did not choose, you're probably caught in a reactive loop. This is a signal that you are not in charge or that you are using your authority inappropriately.

At the beginning of this chapter we looked at the struggle Wayne and Lisa had with their son, Mark. While Mark was extremely manipulative, his parents had one advantage over him: size. They never considered this an asset that they could use. But in doing so, they picked a battle they could win, and they chose the time to fight it. Mark felt the weight of their authority, and he knew he had to yield.

When parents are ineffective, as Lisa and Wayne were, they tend to overestimate or underestimate their power. They discount just how clever and creative children can be in order to get their way. And because kids act with less responsibility than adults, they often win the power struggles, much to their parents' frustration.

Joan was a mother in one of my parenting classes who overestimated her power. She was a controlling, invasive mom whose strategy was to force her children to conform. If they didn't, she felt like a failure. Because she overestimated her power, she was unrealistic about what she could accomplish. She vacillated between gallant but exhausting efforts at control and passive retreats that made her feel inadequate. Trusting God and waiting on him for results in parenting was difficult. All of these shortcomings were magnified when she attempted to toilet train her three-year-old son, Jimmy.

Each time Jimmy was ready to use the toilet, he walked to the bathroom, squatted next to the toilet, and defecated in his pants. This was too much for a controlling mother like Joan, and every episode produced a conflict. As we talked, I sensed that there was more than potty training taking place. I asked her to bring Jimmy to the next class.

During the session, I reviewed the concept of loops and asked Joan to leave the room while Jimmy came in. He took his seat in front of the group and we talked together. I told him that his mom was going to take a new approach.

"And by the way, Jimmy," I asked, "who's the boss in your family?"

"I am," he said without hesitation.

"And what makes you the boss?"

"I'm the boss 'cuz I poop anywhere I want to."

The group laughed and I did my best to keep from joining them as I explained the new system to Jimmy. I agreed with him that he had control over when and where he went to the bathroom. I told him that his mother was not going to argue about using the toilet anymore.

"Jimmy, your mom is the boss. From now on, if you poop in your pants, you'll have to clean up the mess."

"Mom can't make me!" was his only reply.

When Joan returned, I told her about the new strategy and Jimmy's response. Her controller mentality kicked right in.

"We're not going to poop in our pants anymore, are we?" she chided. "Big boys don't poop in their pants, do they?"

The class saw what was happening immediately. Joan was inviting Jimmy into a loop. She overestimated her power and attempted to control Jimmy by cajoling and shaming him. What's more, she wasn't abiding by the new game plan. For the first time, Joan understood it too. Jimmy was more powerful than she realized. She decided she was too vulnerable to initiate the consequences. Even though she saw her weakness and was honest about it, she asked her husband to toilet train Jimmy. Her job was to learn how to disengage from verbal battles for control.

Several months later I received a call from Joan telling me that Jimmy was successfully toilet trained. In actuality, toilet training was not the real problem, only the hot spot; the real problem was a loop that focused on power and who really possessed it. Joan and her husband implemented consequences appropriate to a battle they had to win. They stuck to the hard work required and earned their son's respect—and his cooperation.

Parental Authority

Parental authority is not something everybody enthusiastically supports, especially the "experts." Some psychologists say that hierarchy in the home is the cause of children's problems. Others say that without authority children are guaranteed to struggle. The Bible says that parents are to have authority and use it in an appropriate way. "Children, obey your parents in everything, for this pleases the Lord. Fathers, do not embitter your children, or they will become discouraged" (Col. 3:20–21). Authority is not the culprit. Loops that result from the ineffective or inappropriate use of authority are to blame.

Parental authority is rarely a black-and-white issue. It's not a matter of having total authority or having no authority at all. It's more common to find a mix of potency and impotency in the use of authority. Most of us have acquired our parenting skills from the families in which we were raised. Strengths come from inner security and maturity based on competency and responsibility. But parenting styles are so ingrained that it's difficult to know where our parenting is unhealthy or inefficient. It requires ever-increasing knowledge to discover hidden flaws that weaken our relationships with our children. Knowledge is a reality check on our performance as parents. But what are the standards against which we can measure our exercise of authority?

Healthy authority is expressed by parents who:

1. Make requests
2. Give commands
3. Establish follow-through
4. Are just and fair
5. Are honest
6. Express anger appropriately
7. Trust God and his authority in the child's life
8. Utilize logical and natural consequences that do not endanger the child
9. Establish clear boundaries
10. Allow other authorities to play a corrective role

When these traits are practiced, mothers and fathers are effectively empowered to fulfill their role.

Contrast these skills with the following ineffective strategies. Unhealthy authority is expressed by parents who:

1. Are arrogant in the use of authority

2. Are invasive or intrusive in their dealings
3. Are domineering and self-centered
4. Are unjust, overlooking the contributions of their children
5. Use guilt to manipulate
6. Argue to force compliance
7. Vent anger at the wrong person
8. Call names
9. Verbally or physically abuse
10. Are disrespectful

Each of these actions undermines parental authority and invites self-defeating loops. Some of these actions are judgment calls as to when they cross the line to unhealthy parenting. Be assured, every parent is going to make mistakes, but it's better to risk an error than to shrink from the job you are called to do.

Guidelines for Empowerment

Authority used in a godly way directs your energy toward a godly goal, usually a value that you believe in and want established as an integral part of your family. To accomplish this, your children need a "road map" that shows them how the family is to work and how they can succeed in it. In dysfunctional families there is no map or it is too hard to understand. In this section, we will look at the ten expressions of positive parental authority that will make you more potent in your parenting.

Make Requests

One value that parents desire for their family is cooperation. But many parents seek to force cooperation by yelling or complaining. This usually produces a Demander-Withholder loop. If parents make requests of their child, however, they will create a positive way for the child to contribute to the goal of cooperation.

Requests for cooperation use phrases such as "Would you?" or "Are you willing to?" These are respectful and invite cooperation. If the child agrees to your request, you should expect cooperation. Your follow-through communication can outline your expectation and receive a confirmation from your child. For example: "Great! So I can count on you to have the yard mowed by Saturday afternoon?"

Remember, if you're making requests, the child's cooperation is voluntary. Do not punish if the opportunity is declined.

Make Commands

When a course of action is not a choice and the issue is non-negotiable, a command is appropriate. Make sure the child understands what is expected and that all the parameters of the command are clearly in place. "I expect you to clean up your room by five o'clock" leaves no doubt about the task and the time limit. "You are to do your homework before you go to swimming class" clearly expresses your expectations.

Establish Follow-Through

It is very important to follow through after giving a command, especially with a child who resists. For instance, if you tell your six-year-old to make her bed and she balks, go with her and help her the first time through. This clearly demonstrates your expectation that the task be done, and that it will be her job today and in the future. This creates a healthy atmosphere of cooperation as opposed to threats and warnings with no follow-through attached. These merely demonstrate impotence and lead to arguments and exhaustion.

Be Just

How often has your child said, "That's not fair!"? It's a common rallying cry, particularly for strong-willed children, even though they may not really understand the concept of justice. "Unfair" to the strong-willed child merely means "I didn't get my own way." The child who lives by the motto "Life is not fair!" usually overlooks personal responsibility in creating fairness. Even though the strong-willed child has trouble with the concept, it's valid for parents to consider how they can be just in their parenting.

In family relationships, justice involves reciprocity—the give-and-take between parents and children. In healthy families, parents listen and respond to their children. Everybody's efforts are rewarded, and there is a balance of rewards and responsibilities. In unhealthy families, the opposite is true. Some members are saddled with most of the responsibilities and blame, while others enjoy most of the rewards and privileges. While every family has a mixture of healthy and unhealthy reciprocity, dysfunctional families are decidedly lopsided in their allotment of blame. Like Cinderella in the classic fairy tale, someone carries all the responsibilities but receives none of the rewards. Someone constantly loses, and injustice prevails.

Justice requires that children both learn and experience that their efforts will be rewarded. Conversely, they need to be just and reciprocate in their own relationships. When justice is present in the family, discouragement, frustration, hostility, and loops are minimized. As children adopt the principles of reciprocity they see in their parents, mothers and fathers start to enjoy relationships with their children. And children who realize that rewards and respect are earned and not demanded struggle less with the issue of fairness.

Be Honest

Honesty is an expression of healthy authority. An honest confession of vulnerability can accomplish far more than you realize. Parents don't need to hide behind an inflated image of power to be effective. They can show softness and still maintain authority. For example, if you say, "When you make fun of your sister, it really hurts me," you communicate how your child's actions impact you. You're saying that you expect your child to care about how she affects others and to take personal responsibility for her actions. You can even be honest about discipline. While I'm not suggesting that the old "this is going to hurt me more than it's going to hurt you" cliché is appropriate, there are other honest statements that apply. "I don't enjoy doing this. I'd rather see you happy, but this is my job as a parent," is a truthful way to help a child see things from your perspective.

Honesty bonds you and your child together and keeps you on the same team, even when you exercise authority. If your strong-willed child continues to abuse you when you are honest and vulnerable, you need to begin setting boundaries.

Express Anger

Expressing anger appropriately is key to your success as a parent. Contrary to what some parents believe, anger should not be avoided or ignored. Parents who believe this lack power in their discipline. They also run the risk of not being genuine with their feelings. They're afraid that if they show anger, they'll be hateful or hurtful toward their children.

To be sure, there are hurtful expressions of anger. Anger is inappropriate when it is verbally or physically abusive. Anger is wrong when it is misdirected—for example, if a wife is angry at her husband but takes it out on the children. Anger is misused if it is employed to intimidate or manipulate. And parents of strong-willed children know that it's easy for anger to slip out of control. But the benefits of appropriately expressed anger outweigh these mistakes.

A good rule of thumb is to use your anger to eliminate inappropriate behavior, but to protect the person and the relationship. Used this way, anger can be a barometer, indicating where and when a child is violating boundaries. If anger is viewed as a normal family emotion—in parents and children alike—it is less likely to escalate to inappropriate levels. It also gives you energy and determination to confront behavior, set limits, and stand your ground. And finally, anger can be cleansing if it's not vengeful or punitive.

Healthy families are not uncomfortable expressing anger, but they take responsibility for its effect on each other.

Trust God

Parents who take total responsibility for their strong-willed child's behavior fail to trust God. They assume that they are ultimately responsible for everything in the child's life, and they soon become disrespectful of the child and the relationship with him. They tend to talk at and argue with the child in an effort to maintain control. Conversely, parents who trust God are more able to relax and find security in their roles, even if circumstances or behaviors work against them. Trusting God also allows parents to pick their battles strategically, freeing them from confronting every misbehavior or bad attitude. A parent can only do so much. The rest is up to God and the child. Trust releases a parent's anxiety and depends on God to work as he wills.

Allow Consequences

Parents who trust God allow their children to make choices and experience the consequences. Whether it's allowing natural consequences or implementing logical ones, consequences tap the system God has established to teach children about life. If a child does not eat, the natural consequence is hunger. This puts God squarely on your side if you allow consequences to run their course. Even a strong-willed four-year-old can't fight the God of the universe and win!

If you assume you're the only authority in your child's life, you will usually parent out of worry and fear. This casts you in the role of "bad guy," because the limits you set will be seen by your child as obstacles and not benefits. If you think that you're the only one who can change or shape your child's behavior, any resistance to your authority is serious. You cannot allow space for natural consequences, and a power struggle begins. As the loop increases, a child may throw away common sense and act irrationally simply to win the struggle.

Trusting God to enact logical or natural consequences gives you freedom. Second Timothy 2:25–26 says, "God will grant them repentance leading them to a knowledge of the truth, and that they will come to their senses." God brings the changes. The prodigal son was not changed by his father but by the difficulties his father allowed him to experience. He squandered his inheritance and suffered the natural consequences of poverty and loneliness until God opened his eyes.

One summer my oldest son, who can be very strong-willed, was invited to visit a friend out of state for two weeks. Our relationship was experiencing turbulent times, and I was hesitant to reward him with a trip. But he begged and pleaded until I gave in with the provision that he could go for one week instead of two. He threw a fit. I tried to explain that two weeks was too long, but he continued to badger me. Frankly, he was making the family so miserable that two weeks away didn't sound too bad after all.

"All right," I said, "have it your way. But if you go for two weeks, you'll stay for two weeks."

This established the natural consequences of his decision, and it didn't take long for them to take effect. The phone rang about a week after he left.

"Father, I have sinned against heaven and against you. I am no longer worthy to be called your son." (Just once I'd love to receive a call like that!) Actually, he called to say that he "was lonely and wanted to come home."

"Son, you have another week before you can come back," I said. This time I was firm and willing to let him experience the consequences of his decision.

"Dad, can I call you?" he said with real humility.

Of course my answer was "yes," but it was important that he endured the two weeks for which he begged. He came home with a new attitude. I wasn't the father who wore the "black hat," but the father who simply let him own the consequences of his choices.

Establish Clear Boundaries

Everyone in a family, parents and children alike, needs protection. Boundaries provide guidelines for behavior that protect both you and your children.

Dad may say to his strong-willed child, "It hurts me when you yell at me and call me names." The child responds by saying, "I don't care how you feel. I hate you."

At this point Dad may set a boundary by saying, directly and firmly, "You are not allowed to be mean to any family member and say you hate them. I will not put up with that. You can say you're angry and you don't feel like talking to me, but you are not allowed to be mean."

These kinds of verbal boundaries protect others from hurt and protect the child from feeling guilty. If the child responds by saying, "I can say anything I want and you can't stop me," a follow-through on the boundary is essential. Dad may choose to send the child to her room or give her a time-out. When you are setting boundaries with your strong-willed child, stay away from emotional reactivity. If an argument develops, you can be sure the boundaries are not being respected.

Other Authorities

Sometimes parents need the help of others to implement consequences and wisdom. Parents are often less credible to their children than other authority figures who stand for the same things. It is no shame to have others help you. You are not a failure when you draw on the strength of others: It is a wise parent who uses the resources available to her.

An anxious parent called me one night because his underage child had taken the car and gotten involved in an accident. The police were called, and the father did not know whether to protect his child from the police or take their side.

I said, "Let the police be the 'bad guys' and discipline your child. Call them and tell them you want your child to learn from this, and that you would like them to come over and have a talk with your child about this violation of the law and its consequences. You sit back and let them do the work. You can be the 'good guy' and comfort your child after the police leave." It worked out just fine.

Parenting That Steps over the Line

In the early part of the chapter we focused on parental impotence that results from failing to take charge and implement healthy hierarchy. But parents who attempt to take charge through abusive authority are impotent in their own way. Abusive parents are arrogant, invasive, controlling, and domineering. Each of these abuses results from self-centered, selfish attitudes that are in stark contrast to the Christ-centered, love-based behavior of the Bible.

Love is the force behind potent parenting: "For Christ's love compels us, because we are convinced that one died for all, and therefore all died. And he died for all, that those who live should no longer live for themselves but for him who died for them and was raised again" (2 Cor. 5:14–15). The application to parenting is clear. Jesus died to give us a life that moves us away from selfishness toward serving him. This life will produce parenting full of authority but rich in love. This is godly parenting that focuses on the well-being of the child, not narrow, "me-oriented" power trips. Inappropriate authority is power used only in self-serving ways, which overlooks serving God and others.

Selfishness can usually be traced to a parent's fear and anxiety. For example, some mothers insist their children be perfectly dressed all the time. Every color-coordinated outfit is laid out because they are afraid of being embarrassed. And if—heaven forbid—children should make "creative" choices that mix plaids, stripes, and solids, they force them to change immediately. These mothers are afraid of tarnishing their image, and they can become invasive and domineering.

Self-centered fear also produces authority that is demanding and condemning. This is typified by parents who focus on perfection and performance. Children with parents like this often become frustrated when they can't meet their parents' exacting standards. No matter how hard they try, they fall short. They become discouraged and make half-hearted attempts to satisfy their parents. Parents often misread this frustration as opposition and demand even more.

I have listened to discouraged kids vent their anger at fathers who pointed out the only C on a report card full of A's. The fathers' expectations may have been valid but they were also unrealistic. And the pressure they exerted soon became the problem. As fathers became more exacting, the children became more resistant.

Finally, inappropriate authority produces children who feel smothered. They feel as if their life and personality are being engulfed by parents who dominate and frustrate their pursuit to become individuals. Parents may not realize that a child's efforts to discover identity and purpose are one of the strongest God-given forces in life. Sooner or later, each child needs to be his or her own person, not simply an extension of Mom and Dad. When this desire is frustrated, the natural consequence is rebellion. Unfortunately, rebellion does not free the child at all. Defiance is an emotional reaction, not a healthy assertion of self. As a result, the rebelling child is engulfed in a web of defiant emotions.

Parents who use inappropriate authority with a strong-willed child are sitting on a time bomb. The pastor's child who turns to alcohol or teen pregnancy is emblematic of this struggle. The strong-willed son or daughter may be the most sensitive to feelings of being smothered. If the other children in the family don't rebel, the parent may conclude it's simply a case of having a black sheep in the family and put more controls in place that engulf the child even more. Often the child has to leave the family in order to survive.

When authority is out of control, the abuse can be staggering. Years ago I worked with the Arizona juvenile court system counseling families with children labeled "incorrigible." One family referred to me was extremely religious, but the authority in their home was far from holy.

Mary was fourteen and small for her age. Her shyness made her seem even younger and smaller—a sharp contrast with the court records of her rebellious behavior. The welts and bruises on Mary's body witnessed to her father's belt and metal buckle.

"I can't win in my family," she said meekly. "Everything I do has to be perfect or my father lets me have it."

As we talked about her home, her lip began to quiver, but fear gave way to anger.

"I'm really afraid of him—but I'm angry! I'll never be good enough! And you know what?—I really don't care!"

Mary left my office, and her parents came in. Nobody spoke a word as they passed. David and Karen looked nervous, obviously uncomfortable with having to meet with me. Mary's father made it very clear how he saw the problem.

"If it wasn't for Mary, we'd be a normal family. We wouldn't have to be here," he said with resentment in his voice. "I think she has a demon. She's hateful and mean!"

He watched me closely for my reaction, but I didn't respond.

"Mary gets angry and rebellious. She destroys things in our house," he said, his voice growing louder as he talked. "She *will* submit! I won't put up with this!"

His wife began to cry softly. I confronted David about the abuse he doled out and explained the laws in the state of Arizona.

"'If any man has a stubborn and rebellious son who will not obey his father or mother, they should take him to the city gates and stone him.' Leviticus, I think," he said defiantly. "I'm under God's authority, not the state's!"

"David, is your method of discipline producing godliness in Mary?" I asked.

"No! She's getting worse!" he yelled. "She's going to be just like my mom—a worthless alcoholic, unless I can beat the devil out of her."

David did it all, and he did it all wrong. Over the weeks and months that followed, I saw how he vilified and condemned Mary while he justified himself. He called her the "family devil" and even denied that she was a Christian. After reviewing her files, I knew that Mary wasn't an angel and needed strong parenting. But much of her behavior was simply acting out the role assigned to her by her father.

It took months of court-mandated sessions before David began to see his failings. Raised in an alcoholic family, he had become a Christian but did not put the dynamics of his alcoholic home behind him. The abuse that David foisted on Mary was an expression of his own impotence, and Mary was living out the behavior produced when an abusive parent acts unrestrained.

Building Safety

How safe is your city? Your block? And most importantly, your home?

Has safety been lost because you've succumbed to the tyranny of your strong-willed child? Have you withdrawn in fear or pursued peace at any price? Have you made the mistake that Lisa and Wayne made with Mark, and allowed your child to dictate the rules of your household?

Or are you guilty of driving safety away through selfishness and abuse? Are your children objects against whom you exert inappropriate authority to build your own self-image, importance, and power? Is there a "Mary" in your home who's defiant because of verbal or physical abuse?

Now is the time to evaluate your parenting and the safety that it brings for you and your children. Take a long, hard look at the authority you exercise. It must be firm in order to be effective, but it must be loving in order to be good.

For Your Consideration

1. What do you think are the characteristics of a safe home?
2. What is it that renders you powerless as an authority with your strong-willed child?
3. What do your children do that tells you that they want you to take charge and establish authority?
4. Are you more of a "soft love" or "tough love" parent?
5. What issue in your home is a "battle that you can win"?
6. In what ways do you overestimate your power and underestimate the power of your strong-willed child?
7. In what ways have you underestimated your own power over your child?
8. What healthy authority characteristics are you exercising? What unhealthy characteristics do you need to address?
9. How does your family express anger?
10. What is your greatest weakness in the exercise of authority toward your children?

Skill Builders

Hold the Line. Spend some time thinking about the actions of your strong-willed child that irritate you the most. Determine the line over which the child cannot cross. Determine the consequence if your child crosses the line. When the situation occurs again, explain your plan to your child. Make a six-week commitment to follow through on holding the line and implementing the consequences if your child crosses the line. Take special note to see if this creates order and safety in your home.

Chapter Four

Creating a Positive Family Atmosphere

A happy heart makes the face cheerful,
but heartache crushes the spirit.
Proverbs 15:13

Steve was thirteen years old when he made his debut in court for attempted assault. Brandishing a gleaming steak knife, he had chased his terrified older sister from room to room. Now Steve, his sister Monica, and their panicked mother sat in my study.

Monica folded her arms and glared at me, waiting for me to condemn her brother. But Steve was unmoved and defensive. He shot back angry answers to my questions.

This was not a happy family.

"Tell me more about your relationship with your sister," I said.

Steve rolled his eyes. "So what's to tell? I hate her."

"Then I have a great way for you to get even with her," I said.

Monica's eyes widened, and Steve glumly asked, "How?"

"Love her," I said. "It will drive her nuts."

Steve frowned. Brought up in the church, he'd heard all the "love-talk" he wanted. And yet, Steve didn't tune me out. Raised without a father, he was desperate for other male influences in his life.

"So—how could I love someone like her?" he asked.

For the rest of the session I explained what practical love looked like. I detailed for Steve how Christians are to overcome evil with good, not the other way around. We talked about their patterns of relating, and how they could love instead of hate. Steve actually lis-

67

tened, processing each principle as if it was the first time he'd ever heard such truth.

Best of all, he took it to heart. In just one week, the oppressive, hostile family atmosphere changed. "It's gone from a living hell to heaven, and I don't understand why," his mother said. "But I like it!"

Steve and his sister were locked in a loop that created tension and pervaded every aspect of family life. The loop polluted the atmosphere of the family, and everybody breathed its caustic fumes. When Steve and his sister broke the loop, they began to respond to each other in healthy ways that produced positive feelings.

I wish I could say that breaking the loop brought permanent change to this family. Unfortunately many other problems existed. But for a while, the family atmosphere changed. A fresh breeze blew through their house. With a new emotional tone in the family, they actually began to enjoy each other.

When was the last time you actually enjoyed your family? Along with the effective use of authority, enjoying your family is crucial if you want to build thriving relationships. You can sense whether or not family members enjoy each other by gauging the "family atmosphere," the emotional tone a family establishes that results from how members interact. It reflects the relationships in the family.

Healthy family atmospheres are proactive because each family member focuses on the strengths of the others. They are rewarding places in which to live. Unhealthy family atmospheres are problem-oriented, and members tend to react against each other. They are difficult homes in which to live because family members feel unsuccessful and unappreciated.

One of the most common complaints of parents is that the strong-willed child sets the tone in the family. But the strong-willed child may simply be the one who expresses the anxiety or unhappiness that everyone is feeling. He reflects the family's tension and discomfort. As one teenage boy told me, "When I feel bad on the inside, I act bad on the outside."

Family atmospheres change with life's circumstances. As a result, there is no single ideal family atmosphere. For instance, a healthy family will be serious and reflective when it grieves the loss of a loved one. It would be inappropriate to expect the family to be consistently light and humorous. While it is difficult to generalize family atmospheres, here is a list of "atmospheric conditions" on a scale of 1 to 10. Healthy atmospheres rate closer to 10. Unhealthy atmospheres rate closer to 1. How would each member of your family rate the family atmosphere in your home?

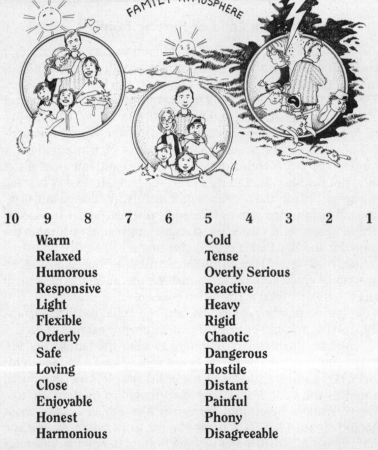

| 10 | 9 | 8 | 7 | 6 | 5 | 4 | 3 | 2 | 1 |

Warm	**Cold**
Relaxed	**Tense**
Humorous	**Overly Serious**
Responsive	**Reactive**
Light	**Heavy**
Flexible	**Rigid**
Orderly	**Chaotic**
Safe	**Dangerous**
Loving	**Hostile**
Close	**Distant**
Enjoyable	**Painful**
Honest	**Phony**
Harmonious	**Disagreeable**

These characteristics vary for every household, but they can help you assess your family atmosphere. Because family members often act out their feelings, evaluating the family atmosphere helps you understand the feelings of everyone involved, especially the strong-willed child.

Family atmosphere is cyclical. While it reflects the dynamics in the home, it also feeds those dynamics. Negative behavior creates a poor family atmosphere, which in turn contributes to more negative behavior. Fortunately, the opposite is true. Once family atmosphere begins to change, it actually encourages positive behavior.

Problem Child or Hurting Family?

Marsha was one of six Parker children and an excellent high school student. But she suffered from depression and pounding, chronic headaches that caused her to retreat from life. The headaches upset Mrs. Parker who put all of her energy into helping Marsha feel better. When Marsha felt good and excelled in school, Mrs. Parker was full of hope for her promising young daughter. When her daughter's headaches came, she attempted to rescue Marsha emotionally and physically. She ended up feeling drained and impotent if she could not help her daughter. As time went on, Mr. Parker became equally concerned, and they consulted their family doctor who diagnosed Marsha's condition as tension headaches. As her headaches grew more severe, Marsha felt responsible for the strain evident in the family. Mr. and Mrs. Parker decided that counseling was the only remedy left. They wanted Marsha's problem "fixed" as soon as possible so their family could get back to normal. We met routinely for several weeks until Mr. Parker's frustration boiled over.

"It's not us who need counseling!" he exclaimed. "It's Marsha who has the problem! The rest of us are unhappy because of her!"

Marsha's depression definitely affected the family, but Mr. Parker's outburst revealed what he felt about Marsha and life in his home. He was angry, and the blame he heaped on Marsha produced heaviness and guilt. Mrs. Parker contributed to the tension, too. When Marsha withdrew into depression, Mrs. Parker worried about her and pursued her. This made Marsha feel smothered, but she didn't know how to share this without hurting her mother's feelings and producing guilt. She chose safe communications instead and focused on the critical attitudes she perceived in her father. The Parkers thought they were a close family, but they were emotionally distant. Their attitudes and actions created an atmosphere full of tension. Everyone contributed to the problem, but they blamed it all on Marsha.

The breakthrough for the Parkers came when their focus changed from "Marsha's problem" to the individual issues each family member carried. In one session, Mr. Parker confessed that he was "very unhappy." He worked hard to be godly and responsible in his job, but the weight of it all produced a high level of stress. What's more, he felt unappreciated, discouraged, and resentful. He expected his wife to make him "feel good" when he came home, but her attention was on Marsha. His honesty helped everybody in the family open up. For the first time, genuine communication created closeness and brought relief to the Parker family.

As each person took responsibility for his or her personal conflicts, tensions steadily decreased. Mr. Parker made changes at work, sought enjoyment beyond just the attention of his wife, and developed a deeper walk with God. Mrs. Parker invested herself in relationships beyond Marsha. This was something she'd always wanted to do, but had never taken time for herself. She also committed to a ministry at church. Soon Marsha's headaches and depression vanished. The Parkers found that enjoyable individual lives produced emotional closeness as a family. And they learned that family atmosphere is more free and enjoyable when each member is more responsible and independent.

The Parkers were caught up in loops when they began counseling. They saw only the day-to-day tension, not the underlying causes, and they blamed their family's problems on Marsha. They overlooked their own feelings and failed to take personal responsibility for them. Mr. Parker's stress and burnout affected Marsha's headaches. Marsha's depression impacted her mother who kept pursuing and trying to rescue her. When Marsha felt her mother was invading her life, she withdrew further and her sadness increased. Everyone played a part in creating the tense family atmosphere, but the symptoms showed up most prominently in Marsha.

Stress and Overload

Much tension in a family atmosphere is the result of stress. To be sure, stress is a part of life. Jesus guaranteed it when he said, "In this world you will have trouble" (John 16:33). During times of stress, the family as a whole and its individual members wrestle to maintain equilibrium. Too often one person is pushed beyond his limits and experiences greater problems. This is often the strong-willed child, who feels the pressure more keenly and reacts more dramatically than more compliant children. Other family members may vent their frustration at the strong-willed child's emotional behavior. While pointing the finger may relieve their stress, it confirms the impression that the strong-willed child is the one who is increasing everyone's anxiety and creating conflict.

The families who suffer most during stressful times are those who possess high levels of anxiety or are emotionally enmeshed. When circumstances destroy their equilibrium, the most sensitive and emotionally dependent child in the family—in most families the strong-willed child—actively demonstrates his hurt, sometimes by acting out in anger. Parents may try to rescue the child out of the nervousness they feel about his behavior. If they restore the child's emotional balance, they temporarily ease the pressure. Unfortunately, rescuing the child may not build emotional independence or maturity.

Times of trouble and stress can come from events like the birth of a child or the addition of children through remarriage. Stress results when children leave home or when emotional separation occurs in adolescence. Even the failure of a child to live up to a parent's expectations can create stress. Anything that changes or disrupts the equilibrium of the family is a potential stress producer. How a family handles it is crucial.

Loss is another great producer of stress. If the loss is major, like the death of a child, divorce, or bankruptcy, it can overload the system. When households function well, the members talk about their feelings and comfort each other. They are independent but loving. They facilitate the grieving process rather than block it.

While loss can be one of life's most painful experiences, a family's response to anxiety and method of coping can create additional problems. Hurting, needy families can turn on each other if they feel affection is being withheld or comfort denied. Their anger and resentment can create a hostile atmosphere if they feel desperate for comfort but cannot find it. Some will find comfort by distancing themselves emotionally. Others will make emotional connections to cope. And some will vent emotions to find release. It is also likely that pain and anxiety will lead to one family member being treated as the scapegoat.

When family members have a healthy emotional independence, they are free to find love and comfort outside the family and bring that comfort home. They ask for help and find it in God and other healthy sources like support groups, pastors, counselors, and friends. They avoid sources of comfort that increase pain and alienation like drugs and alcohol. They are cautious of overeating, overspending, or becoming trapped in unhealthy relationships. And they are realistic in their dependence upon the family. They don't expect their family to meet every need, and so they are less demanding and feel less desperation during times of grief. These families help each other face the hard realities of loss in order to find strength and courage.

Finally, stress comes from too many demands and pressures, unpleasant surprises, too little space, overstimulation, or too little rest from our labors. Overload causes families to overreact or become guarded and rigid when they feel imposed upon. Overloaded families treat each other disrespectfully, even though the enemy is stress, not the family itself.

Stress is a powerful enemy of healthy family atmosphere. When family members take personal responsibility for recovering from stress and establish respectful boundaries, family atmosphere improves. Tension will diminish when families face stress head-on, learn how to relax, and trust God in the midst of pressures. This doesn't mean anxiety goes away, but healthy families deal with it so that it will not control the family.

The Overly Serious Family

A family's attitude toward life can often produce more anxiety and pain than the difficulties the family faces. Emotionally mature families foster attitudes, beliefs, and behaviors that enable its members to handle stress successfully. Less mature families model attitudes, beliefs, and behaviors that are detrimental. This is especially true when families are overly serious. Anxiety colors the family atmosphere and tension flows like electricity to an outlet. When stress occurs, a connection is made and someone (or maybe the whole family) is "shocked" by the flow of negative emotions. This is less likely to occur when a family relaxes and develops a sense of humor.

ANXIETY - DRIVEN

Seriousness is not a sin. Families who aren't serious about their responsibilities will not establish the order and safety a home requires. But some families go too far. They have no sense of humor and are unable to play. They are rigid and obsessed with problems. Life's minor issues become catastrophes.

Donna had three children, the oldest of whom had numerous learning disabilities. Years of fighting for appropriate education and treatment for her son had left Donna pessimistic and suspicious. She expected the worst from every situation. Donna's face registered continual tension; she never smiled. Now her youngest, three-year-old Stacy, had entered a strong-willed phase, and Donna was on the verge of collapse. Every battle Stacy waged—from refusing to put on socks to running away in the grocery store—caused Donna to overreact.

The real culprit in Donna's family was not her son's disabilities or even her daughter's confrontations, but seriousness and anxiety. Donna couldn't see that her overly serious approach to life was contributing to Stacy's behavior. Donna identified and reacted to "problems" to which more relaxed families would never give a second thought.

Christians should have a decided advantage when it comes to facing adversity. When Christian families believe that God is good and sovereign, they can relax emotionally. Jesus' Sermon on the Mount could be titled "Don't Worry, Be Happy." If I summarized a section of this marvelous discourse of Christ for the overly serious family, I would say, "Relax! Chill out. God cares for you and will meet your needs. Being anxious will not help!" Problems are going to come, but Jesus encouraged his followers to avoid the stress and futility of worry when he said, "Therefore do not worry about tomorrow, for tomorrow will worry about itself. Each day has enough trouble of its own" (Matt. 6:34).

What does this approach to life look like? For families who know how to relax, it means they can play with each other through a good-natured sense of humor. Humor helps them make positive connections that result in warm, friendly feelings. It is humor that is pure and avoids sarcasm, a cover for anger. When family members help each other feel good through play instead of trying to change or anxiously take responsibility for each other, the atmosphere lightens.

Joe and Brenda were caught in a Controller-Rebel loop. Brenda's low commitment to housekeeping was upsetting Joe, and she was becoming increasingly frustrated with his anger. The more he insisted on a clean house, the more disinterested Brenda became in the task. The neatness of their house was becoming a source of contention. In one of our sessions I suggested that the problem was not the house but the seriousness of their responses toward each other. They needed to find a way to "play" amid a circumstance that was becoming a major battleground. If they diffused their anxious responses, their whole relationship might improve. I sent them home with that specific challenge. A few weeks later they reported on their progress.

"Joe came home Tuesday night, and one look at the house was all it took," Brenda said. "He was angry and I could feel the tension starting to rise. As quickly as I could I dropped to one knee, hung my head and pleaded, 'Master, Master, please forgive me!' I looked up and smiled. We both broke into laughter and haven't been the same since."

There's a Christian saying that says, "Laugh at the devil, and he will flee from you." Joe and Brenda will tell you it's true.

Therapists call a radical change in directions like this a paradox. Jesus used paradox with his followers when he commanded them to love their enemies—something that probably seemed absurd until they actually obeyed. Moving your overly serious family toward playfulness and humor may take a miracle, but God is in the miracle business. Ask him for grace, and he'll supply what you need. It may seem absurd to think that your family can move in a new, lighter direction. The change, however, will break the tension. And don't be surprised if God uses your strong-willed child to make this playful transition. The strong-willed child often has a keenly developed sense of humor. His or her propensity to take life less seriously than you can be helpful in breaking tension for everyone.

Toting Heavy Baggage

Sometimes the heaviness encountered in families goes beyond the immediate situation. It comes from emotional baggage packed by the family in which a parent was raised and passed down through several generations. Baggage produces heaviness because it loads a situation with old emotions that are not appropriate to the situation at hand. Until it's dealt with, relationships will be short-circuited. I've seen a mother explode and become resentful because her son failed to take out the trash. The emotional baggage she carried, however, was the memory of her irresponsible father who walked out on his family for another woman. Her response had far more behind it than was apparent.

Andrea exemplifies what baggage can do. Andrea was a controlling mother who overprotected her child. She was anxious about his welfare and plagued by reoccurring fears that he would die. But behind her anxiety was the grief of five children lost to miscarriage before her son was born. In addition to the weight of her personal baggage, Andrea's mother lost a son while he was a small boy. The family never talked about it and Andrea never grieved the loss. What's more, Andrea didn't connect her anxiety and control to the past losses. Baggage like this—even if it's not talked about, acknowledged or consciously known—colors the emotional atmosphere in the family until it's unloaded.

Sharon carried in her emotional baggage as she and her ten-year-old stepson, George, came for counseling, prompted by his behavior problems at school. Sharon's husband was an immigrant who had few marketable skills and earned minimum wage. That forced her to become the family's chief financial supporter. In addition to financial pressures, her husband brought five children from a previous marriage into the home.

But Sharon herself was no stranger to adversity.

She grew up in a "religious" home with an unstable mother and an emotionally distant father. Each Sunday her mother saw to it that all the children attended church with her. Her religion, however, did not prevent her from having several affairs during her married life—affairs that she described to Sharon! Sharon worked hard to stabilize the family and assumed a huge amount of responsibility in light of her parents' instability. Her tendency to overfunction in her childhood home was alive and well in her new household. The problem evidenced itself in the growing loop between Sharon and her stepson.

When Sharon felt George was making her life too difficult, she became angry and expressed it by distancing herself from him emotionally. When George felt cut off, he went through several stages of reaction. His initial hurt turned into anger, which he acted out in school. Sharon was a good student as a child, so George's misbehavior at school upset her even more. All of this was compounded by the fact that George lost his birth mother at age six, and he actually bonded strongly with Sharon. When she distanced herself, it brought back all his feelings of loss and abandonment and left him sulking around the house. All of this conspired to make the relationship between Sharon and George heavy and tense. As we began counseling, neither one was able to disengage emotionally. Each of them reacted to the other and was dependent on the other's response. While I counseled them together, I also spent individual time to help them deal with their emotional baggage so they could communicate and love each other more freely.

During one of our joint sessions, the tension was thick between George and his stepmother. Both of them were angry as they came into the room, but neither would talk about it until I pushed the issue.

"George blew it at school again!" Sharon finally admitted.

George hung his head and began to cry. Based on what I knew of George's strong bond with Sharon, I made an observation.

"You must love your stepmother very much," I said.

George simply nodded and the tears continued to flow.

Sharon was incredulous. She glared at me and then squared off toward George.

"If you love me so much," she charged, "then why do you hurt me?"

"Because you hurt me!"

"George," I said, "do you know how you hurt your mom?"

"School—I do bad things at school," he sniffed.

"George, what do you think God wants you to do?" I asked.

George thought for a moment and lifted his head toward Sharon.

"I'm sorry, Mom. Would you forgive me for hurting you?"

Sharon began to weep but did not speak.

"Sharon, you need to respond to George's apology," I said.

The atmosphere was beginning to change to a softer, peaceful tone. Sharon took a deep breath and looked at George.

"Yes, George, I do forgive you."

"Sharon," I asked, "do you know how you hurt George?"

"No. I really don't know," she said with a tone of exasperation. "I try so hard to be a good mom and I still fail!"

"Tell her. Tell her how she hurts you," I said to George.

"You won't talk to me! You don't look at me. You don't hug me anymore and it hurts me! It hurts bad," George sobbed.

Sharon started to defend herself but stopped and turned her full attention to George. With a heart of sincerity she said, "George, I'm sorry. Would you forgive me?"

"Yes, Mom. Yes I will," George replied, and they moved across the room for a moment of quiet embrace. Sharon and George let go of the heaviness in their relationship and released resentments. They experienced the healing that comes from honesty, cleansing past hurts, and unloading emotional baggage.

When families pursue honesty and forgiveness, they become responsible. They work through underlying feelings so that the family atmosphere loses its heaviness. A new, lighter tone brings emotional freedom for everybody.

Secrets and Power

One of the most popular TV shows of the 1950s was "I've Got A Secret." It was fun to guess the special secrets each guest owned. But secrets in the family aren't anything like the old TV show. Family secrets cover up alcoholism, sexual abuse, and other acts that would bring shame if they were known. Family secrets stifle family atmosphere and rob it of freedom and joy.

When I talk about strong-willed children, however, the secrets I refer to are the discussions family members have about the "bad kid" and the problems she has. They are secrets because they exclude the strong-willed child. The family members who have the discussion are "in power" because they share "privileged information"— information that the strong-willed child is not allowed to hear. This is precisely where the problem occurs.

Quite often, the strong-willed child tyrannizes those "in power" because she feels powerless. If she simply had the information about her behavior that the family was discussing, she would be in a better position to grow and behave correctly. She does not receive it, however, because she tends to react and become defensive. It's also true that the family has its own weaknesses. They can be fearful, angry, and react with emotion, too. All of this creates a cycle in which honesty is difficult. The secrets continue and the strong-willed child feels left out, alienated, and the object of gossip. The schism creates family tension that yearns for reconciliation.

The Bible clearly teaches that honesty must be expressed in love, gentleness, and humility (Eph 4:15; Gal. 6:1). A positive family atmosphere allows family secrets to be revealed with honesty and an assurance of safety. Parents who seek to create such an atmosphere will need to press on to maturity in their relationship with Christ. They might need help from someone outside the family, like a pastor, counselor, or trusted friend—who can facilitate without being anxious and reactive. But by all means, parents need to end family secrets that create unhealthy alliances. Honesty is risky and uncomfortable. The strong-willed child may react negatively to what she hears. But if family members, including the strong-willed child, act responsibly, tension can diminish and family relationships can grow.

Enjoying Your Family

Despite your past experience, your family can be a potential source of enjoyment and motivation, just as God intended. He created it to be a place where each family member finds pleasure and rest. Families are to be rewarding places that inspire. This doesn't mean parents are to live to make children happy and reward their every effort. This is both impossible and unhealthy. But consistent efforts toward making your family an enjoyable place to be are important in producing health and hope for its members.

Don't be deceived about family atmosphere. It is not a Pollyanna wish for a pain-free family. God promises that life contains suffering and disappointment. Realistically, families will be a source of enjoyment at some times and a source of pain at others. The good news is that God is redemptive in our sin and suffering. He brings good things out of bad situations. What appears to be a failure at one point in your family's life can become an asset later on. As in Joseph's story of family rejection and loss, God uses pain and hurts for good. After years of struggle and adversity, Joseph was able to say to his brothers, "You intended to harm me, but God intended it for good" (Gen. 50:20).

Enjoying your family is not denying pain, but discovering how God will enable you to work through it. This is what many self-help books miss. They promise complete healing and deny that difficulties are an ongoing part of life. If you believe their promises, you will be disillusioned. In truth, a healthy family atmosphere is one where family members are simply complaining less and focusing more on God and eternal values. They work together, play together, and help each other succeed in their individual purposes in life despite pain and setbacks.

One reason healthy families succeed is their ability to recognize and validate individual effort. They understand that if they stifle, ignore, or punish a child for honest effort, the results will be oppressive. Healthy families wisely blend common sense and good manners when a child does well or tries hard. And they see recognition pay off handsomely.

An easy way to reward effort is simply to say "thank you," or "I appreciate that." Combining compliments with love is effective. Saying, "I really appreciate you. The job you did on the family room looks great!" combines love and praise. Parents who recognize their child's efforts and give positive strokes will see the child's spirit thrive. Look for areas to praise. When your child does well on a test, puts effort into household chores, or tries hard to be loving, your acknowledgment and validation can make a huge impact.

Simple courtesy and mutual respect build a healthy atmosphere. When each person respects and honors what's important to the other, life is more meaningful and relationships more enjoyable. There is a Swedish proverb that says "a shared joy is twice the joy; a shared sorrow is half the sorrow." It's true.

Families that do not function well communicate negative feelings and don't reward their children. These families enter no-win situations. A father complains that his child "never does his homework." If the child promises to do better, his father may say, "Don't bother. It won't make any difference anyway." The child can't win. If he doesn't do the homework, it will upset his father. If he does the homework, his father discounts the effort. This is a no-win transaction that produces confusion, hurt, and frustration. It makes the family negative and unrewarding.

Families with a strong-willed child are especially susceptible to this negative pattern. Because so many interactions with a strong-willed child are difficult, parents may begin to expect him to fail. They don't expect him to do his homework, and if he tries, he does it poorly. The parents expect to be disappointed and, of course, they are. The child doesn't do the homework because he fears his parents' condemnation. The parents and child are trying to protect themselves from hurt, but no one is successful. They are locked in a no-win situation with pain being the only reward.

Parents must be willing to pay the price to break the pattern—a price that will require commitment, short-run pain, and work. When homework is due, Mom or Dad will need to insist on its completion but do so without caustic comments on how well they think the child will do. When the assignment is done, nonconstructive criticism must be avoided. The child's work may not be outstanding, and this may be painful for the parents. But the child must see that the effort of completing the assignment will be rewarded for its own sake. Over time, the simple appreciation of a job completed can grow to a reward for a job well done. The important thing is to eliminate reactive loops that produce no-win situations. Mom and Dad must be less dependent on the child's positive response and the quality of work and more dependent on God to help them respond appropriately. As old patterns and expectations are erased and new ones are built, family members will begin to enjoy one another.

A Place to Belong

The strong-willed child needs a place to belong, a place that comes from a positive role in the family. In most homes with a strong-willed child, this positive place is missing and the child feels empty, frustrated, and alienated. He acts out these feelings of powerlessness and tyrannizes the family with unacceptable behavior. Parents don't see weakness, however. They encounter a powerful child who in their eyes controls the atmosphere of the whole family. The child needs a new role in which he can make positive contributions and build the family atmosphere. If he doesn't receive it, even the few positives in his life can be lost.

John was a strong-willed child whose only positive strokes came on the soccer field. At home he struggled with obedience and acted out his bad feelings through rebellion. His parents felt trapped. They enjoyed the fact that he excelled in soccer, but they felt they were rewarding his behavior by allowing him to continue to play the game he loved. Since soccer was the only thing their son cared about, they thought that losing the privilege might influence John to change. They took him off the team.

Unfortunately, they took away the only constructive avenue in which their son made a positive contribution and the only place where he felt a positive sense of belonging. They did not understand that when a child has difficulty finding a place to belong in the family, he or she will antagonize from a position of alienation. This opposition causes the few positive places in life to be taken away. Instead of solving the problem, John's parents intensified it.

A little girl was watching her mother wash clothes at the laundromat. "Can I put some clothes in, Mommy?" she pleaded. "Can I add the soap?" "Can I help you fold the towels?"

Each request increasingly annoyed her mother. "Stop pestering me," she snapped. "I'm too busy to have you mess up the laundry."

The little girl sat down dejectedly on a plastic chair against the wall until a mischievous look spread across her face. She hopped from the chair and slid stealthily to another laundry cart. She quickly reached in, took an item of clothing, and darted out the door, her mother chasing after her. She found a way to belong!

In homes with both a strong-willed and a compliant child, the one who cannot be the best at being good becomes the best at being bad. The strong-willed child may be a born antagonist, but the innate differences between the "good" and the "bad" child are often exaggerated. This can lead both children into rigid roles and life scripts that are not necessarily healthy. If parents can find ways to invite the strong-willed child to gain a sense of belonging, they can break the rigid role in which he is trapped.

Jesse's older sister was just about perfect and he knew it. On the other hand, he was the tyrant in his family and his church, which was quite an accomplishment to achieve by age eight. Some of the congregation even suggested that he was demon possessed because of the "look in his eye" and the mean things he did. His parents believed they could curb his behavior through spanking, and they sometimes spanked him up to twenty times a day. Everybody was emotionally exhausted from the constant confrontation.

One day Jesse badgered his mother and she warned him to stop. When he didn't back-off she yelled, "If you don't stop, I'm going to spank you!" Without missing a beat Jesse started in again. After all the spankings and all the confrontations, Jesse's mother was spent. She actually began to chuckle and said to her husband, "No wonder parents feel powerless!"

That night Jesse's mother and father decided their strategies were not working. Spankings alone were not the answer. They were tired of focusing on Jesse's poor behavior and explored some of the positive aspects of his life. What did Jesse do well? What were his gifts and talents besides creating chaos? What activities did he benefit from that they could support? They realized that he was an aspiring athlete and that he also did well in several subjects in school. They began to encourage these strengths with him. At first he was hesitant to accept a positive role in the family. His self-identity was that of the rebel. Over a period of time, however, Jesse developed into an outstanding athlete and became a source of pride to himself and his family. They actually began to enjoy spending time together. Even the people in church were amazed when they saw the positives in his life and realized the "demons" of his childhood were gone.

What About Your Family?

"You can pick your friends, but you can't pick your family," the old saying goes. And since you are all in this together, the atmosphere of your family is important. I want you to ask yourself, "Does every member of my household find the family a rewarding place to be?" Is it a family filled with tension or one that is safe and relaxed? Some families today are so gloomy and stormy that children wish their parents would die. One man I counseled told me that he spent his childhood wishing his father would be killed on his way home from work. And some parents look forward to the day when their children leave home for good. As one mother said, "I've had enough of this child and her tyranny. I could easily divorce her from my life!"

Family atmospheres can be deadly or they can be life-giving. What will your children remember about your home? Will it be like the remembrances this daughter shared in a letter with her father?

Dear Dad,

I have learned so much from you in my childhood. I have watched you for many years and have the utmost respect for you and the character you have worked to develop. As I have reflected on my life, I remember many moments when you touched my life because of your laughter and great sensitivity. I think what I am trying to say is thank you for being such a unique dad and teaching me so much. You've been a wonderful parent and hero to me. I love you very much.

That's family atmosphere at its best.

For Your Consideration

1. Where does your family focus more: on its strengths or weaknesses?
2. How would you describe the family atmosphere in your house? (Stormy, partly cloudy, or sunny?)
3. Do members of your family take personal responsibility for their feelings or do they tend to blame others?
4. During times of stress, does your family turn to healthy or unhealthy sources of comfort? What are they?
5. In what areas does your family tend to be overly serious?
6. In what ways do your and your spouse's past unresolved emotional issues contribute to current loops in your family?
7. Does your strong-willed child have a positive role in your family in which she can contribute? What is it? How could you help her develop one?
8. Is your family a rewarding or unrewarding place to be for every family member? Why or why not?

Skill Builders

Adjust the Family Barometer. Identify an area in your family that is neither safe nor enjoyable. Talk with family members about this area by asking questions. Discover what they think and how they feel about it. What would make them feel safe in this area or what could make it more enjoyable? Discuss together how you are going to work toward these goals and ask them to do their part to make it safe and enjoyable.

Example: At dinner time, family members are always late, and they complain and fight when Mom asks them to help with tasks. When the mother considers taking charge of this area, she realizes she hasn't defined her expectations or asked for cooperation. She and the rest of the family are simply reacting to chaos and resistance.

She initiates a discussion with the whole family and asks them whether or not they enjoy the dinner hour. Most of them do not. She asks them how it could be improved. As she listens to their ideas, she asks them to commit to their suggestions and defines her own set of expectations as well as the consequences for failing to meet them. ("Dinner will be served at 6:00. If you are late, you will not eat with us.") She doesn't argue, but she does take charge. Over time, the family atmosphere at dinner will improve with everybody's effort.

Chapter Five

Finding the Balance

The law was added so that the trespass might increase.
But where sin increased, grace increased all the more.

Romans 5:20

How can children be so different?

In the same house, with the same parents, two sons can live diametrically opposed lives. One is the "good kid"—the conforming child who plays by the rules. He understands your beliefs and you appreciate his cooperation. Then there's the strong-willed child, the one you secretly consider your "bad kid" There isn't a rule that he considers binding. Your values have as much impact on him as a feather hitting stones. When these two get together, sparks fly. God knows about brothers like these.

> Now Abel kept flocks, and Cain worked the soil. In the course of time Cain brought some of the fruits of the soil as an offering to the Lord. But Abel brought fat portions from some of the firstborn of his flock. The Lord looked with favor on Abel and his offering, but on Cain and his offering he did not look with favor. So Cain was very angry, and his face was downcast.
>
> Then the Lord said to Cain, "Why are you angry? Why is your face downcast? If you do what is right, will you not be accepted? But if you do not do what is right, sin is crouching at your door; it desires to have you, but you must master it."
>
> Now Cain said to his brother Abel, "Let's go out to the field." And while they were in the field, Cain attacked his brother Abel and killed him.

Then the Lord said to Cain, "Where is your brother Abel?"

"I don't know," he replied. "Am I my brother's keeper?"

The Lord said, "What have you done? Listen! Your brother's blood cries out to me from the ground. Now you are under a curse and driven from the ground, which opened its mouth to receive your brother's blood from your hand. When you work the ground, it will no longer yield its crops for you. You will be a restless wanderer on the earth."

Cain said to the Lord, "My punishment is more than I can bear. Today you are driving me from the land, and I will be hidden from your presence; I will be a restless wanderer on the earth, and whoever finds me will kill me."

Gen. 4:2–14

Cain and Abel is an extreme story of the "good kid" and "bad kid." It is the story of God's system of sacrifice and what was acceptable. Cain's gift didn't fit, and he felt the sting of rejection and alienation. What's more, he felt the loss of acceptance in stark contrast to the favor God showed Abel.

Cain had a choice. He could acknowledge God's system, conform to it and gain a sense of belonging, or he could rebel. Cain's anger twisted his will, and in the field from which he gleaned his unacceptable sacrifice, he murdered his brother. Abel became the ultimate scapegoat. Cain created a future of alienation and wandering. He became the loser, the loner, and the son who blamed others for the misery in his life.

Here's the shocker. Cain felt no different than the strong-willed child in your house. He felt rejected and without value. He doubted his efforts would ever be good enough. He convinced himself that everybody else was wrong. And he felt different from everybody else around him.

But God's system wasn't going to change. Cain needed repentance. He needed to conform to the values and standards that God established so he could experience a sense of belonging.

So who was right? Was God too severe in his rejection of Cain? Or was Cain naive to expect that he could live life on his own terms? The answer is important for families today.

Every household has a system of beliefs and values. For many children, acceptance only comes if they do what is expected. If they conform, they are loved. If they rebel, they are the outcasts. The values and beliefs of the system define relationships instead of relationships defining the system. It's a complex and delicate subject, but it can mean the difference between unity and division in your home.

You Have a System

Families establish values, standards, and goals to define themselves and their relationships. You might think Christian families share identical goals because the Bible is their basis for truth. But just as there are tremendous differences in denominations and churches, there are also great distinctions in families. Some families emphasize home schooling or Christian education to strengthen family life and build separation from the world. Some value athletics and the importance of discipline, achievement, and winning. In my own family, we value relationships and our individual gifts and talents. We strive together to know God and be good students, athletes, and friends.

Take a few minutes to think about your own family system. What kinds of interests and activities do you tend to gravitate toward as a family? What adjectives describe how you tackle family projects? What values do you uphold above all others? What values and beliefs do you hope your children will pass on to their children?

Whatever the emphases, families value their beliefs and structure because these things give them significance. They provide security and a place to belong. Families are encouraged when their values are supported and threatened when they are challenged. The system is central and defines whether or not a family member "fits" and contributes.

But problems arise when the family system is too rigid. In strict, unyielding systems, family members feel excluded when they do not conform. The more distant they feel from the family's core beliefs, the less they adopt those standards for themselves. They become nonconformists and contribute little to the family system.

The Child Who Just Doesn't Fit

No one will argue that families should live without beliefs and values. Children need to understand what is important and how to conform. Opposing authority hurts the child and the family.

It's important, therefore, that parents explain their beliefs and what they expect from their children. Defining the system is important. In the Old Testament, the Mosaic law defined the rights and wrongs of Israel's relationship with God. But defining the system does not empower people to live up to it. It does not eliminate problems or change a person's behavior. This is precisely what Paul says about the law in Romans 3:20–22:

THE SQUARE-PEG FAMILY

"No one will be declared righteous in [God's] sight by observing the law; rather, through the law we become conscious of sin. But now a righteousness from God . . . comes through faith in Jesus Christ to all who believe."

The same is true in families. Families should define their beliefs and values, but the explanation alone will not ensure that everyone in the family will conform. In fact, for the strong-willed child, defining the family system may give her more concrete ideas on how to rebel against that system!

Does this mean you should ignore your beliefs and values and encourage family members to develop their own ideas? Not at all. Your family needs definition, and members need to conform to your goals and purposes in order to feel that they have a contribution to make. Problems occur when a family moves beyond defining their system to setting it in stone. The system becomes more important than its members. This is exactly what happened in Old Testament Israel. Thank God he provided a new system: grace.

Law and Grace

While a discussion of law and grace may seem more appropriate for Sunday morning, these two concepts have much to say about your family system. In law-oriented families, the focus is on goals and standards. Parents find it hard to trust God to develop a healthy, functional family. Rules take priority over relationships, and the family is cold and mechanical. In grace-oriented families, individuals are important, and parents strive to trust God with the process of growth. They trust him with the process of instilling values in their children that enable them to contribute to a vital, functioning family.

Many parents are at odds over law and grace. Often one parent is a nurturer who emphasizes relationships while the other emphasizes performance and conformity. If the nurturing parent dominates, children feel safe but may not be challenged to grow. If the parent who expects performance and conformity dominates, children grow but feel insecure. In extreme cases, the parents actually neutralize each other.

Individuals and family systems are equally important. If you eliminate or minimize either one, the family suffers. The challenge is how to deal with nonconformity and individuality—your strong-willed child's unique nature—and still maintain a healthily functioning family. Grace provides the answer.

Grace Promotes Relationships

At ten years old, Sally and Jenny were best friends. They went to the same church, where Jenny's father was pastor, and spent all their time together at school. Sally and Jenny decided it was time to "grow up." In their minds, the best way to start was to forsake the "little girl look" and start using makeup. They stopped at a store after school and fastidiously experimented with their new look. They went home to model the results.

"What do you think you're doing?" Sally's mother yelled. "You look like a slut!" She grabbed Sally by the arm and forced her into the bathroom. Sally felt assaulted as her mother harshly wiped away her carefully applied makeup.

Down the street, Jenny's father looked up from the mail and did a double take at the sight of eyeliner and lipstick. He felt threatened by the sudden new look.

"Jenny," he said after some routine small talk, "I can't help but notice the makeup you're wearing. I have to confess, it makes me uncomfortable. I'm just not sure your mother and I are ready for makeup at your age. Will you do one thing for me?"

Jenny was apprehensive, but didn't feel attacked. "Well what do you have in mind?" she asked.

"All I'm asking is that you pray about this. What do you think God would have you do about makeup at your age?"

That seemed fair to Jenny. Her father didn't look angry and wasn't yelling. Praying about it wasn't too much to ask, she thought.

That night, Jenny struggled in prayer. She wanted to do the right thing, but she enjoyed the grown-up feeling makeup gave her.

The next day Jenny told her father she could wait for lipstick and eyeliner. Her decision relieved him, but the fact that their relationship did not suffer pleased him even more. The same wasn't true in Sally's house. Sally and her mother weren't speaking.

Sally's mother used legalism to punish her child for breaking the rules of the system. A family value—makeup is sinful—was more important than Sally's perfectly normal desire to feel grown up. Sally's mother heaped on condemnation, guilt, and force to shame her daughter into compliance. In her zeal for obedience, she abused her relationship with Sally, who withdrew in anger and resentment. Sally wasn't wearing makeup, but she wasn't repentant either. The law ruled, and the consequence was separation.

Strong-willed children with law-oriented parents become quickly frustrated in their attempts to get their own way. They will eventually seek friends outside the family who support their nonconformity. Resentment toward their families grows. Parents become increasingly nervous as they feel rejected by their children. They criticize their children's newfound friends to the point that relationship breaks down altogether.

Jenny's father saw things differently. He decided to let go of the makeup issue and trust God to work in the situation. Jenny changed because her father allowed her to think, pray, and make her own decision. Even if Jenny decided that lipstick was permissible, he committed himself to deal with her respectfully. He presented his standards and beliefs while he pursued relationship and dialogue.

Grace Promotes Responsibility

Roger and Beth Meyers left their children with a sitter while they went out for the evening with friends. They came home to disaster. Their six-year-old son Charlie had thrown a screaming tantrum, repeatedly kicking and hitting the babysitter and, in the process, tearing her blouse. She had called her father who arrived to restore order and left when Charlie was under control in his room.

After Roger took the sitter home and apologized for Charlie's behavior, he raced back to deal with his son. He vowed he'd never leave Charlie alone again and hurried up the stairs to his son's room.

"What's the matter with you, you little punk?" he shouted. "Are you some kind of animal? When I leave this house, the sitter is in charge, and I expect you to act like a human being!"

Roger's rage was skyrocketing. He shouted insults and threats at his terrified son. Beth stepped between them to calm things down, but Roger pushed her away with a strong forearm. He piled on shame until Charlie's guilt overwhelmed him and Roger satisfied his anger. When Roger went to bed, Beth called their family counselor who promised to contact her husband the next day.

In the morning, Roger told the counselor what happened and said Charlie apologized. "But has Charlie changed?" the counselor asked. "Is he repentant or is he just sorry he had the conflict with you?"

"I don't know," Roger said. "Charlie apologized, but said the babysitter started the whole thing anyway."

The counselor thought about the past dynamics of this family. He concluded that Charlie's remorse was not repentance. Charlie was used to being condemned by his father. He coped by thinking, "You can yell at me all you want. I deserve it, but I'm not going to change."

"This situation isn't finished," the counselor said. "Charlie needs to go to the babysitter's house and apologize in person."

"That seems like a lot of work," Roger said. "Besides, Charlie told me he was sorry when I punished him last night."

"If this is the kind of behavior you want, don't take him," the counselor said. "But if you want Charlie to take responsibility for his actions, he needs to apologize face-to-face and make amends."

Two days later, Roger enthusiastically reported on Charlie's visit with the babysitter. Charlie apologized personally and offered to pay for the blouse. The sitter declined the offer, but accepted the apology. She even agreed to sit for the Meyers again.

More importantly, Charlie's father learned that condemnation and shame do not teach responsibility. Charlie needed a relationship with his father that moved him to accountability. Roger's anger made Charlie feel guilty and worthless, but not repentant. When Roger moved away from the law, he took a firm but loving step toward making Charlie responsible and mature. It was an important first step in grace.

Grace Provides Unconditional Love

Liz was a teenager who grew up in a conservative Lutheran home in the Midwest. When she went away to college, her already strained relationship with her parents worsened. She took extra measures to separate herself from their values. She dyed her hair purple, dressed in black, and absorbed herself in heavy-metal music. Her parents worried, and her weekend visits were awkward and painful.

Her parents finally decided that unconditional love was the only way to maintain their relationship with their daughter. On one weekend visit, they went out to dinner and spent the evening probing and listening to Liz's beliefs without overreacting or condemning her. Their openness surprised her, and she even explained why her parents' beliefs were difficult for her to believe.

It was enlightening for Liz's parents to hear her thoughts, even if they were difficult to accept. And Liz felt more freedom and safety with her parents than she ever had before. In the warmth of the moment, Liz asked to stay out late and her parents said yes. The family left the restaurant on a rare, emotional high.

All that changed the next morning. Liz came home at 4 A.M., and her parents spent the night angry and afraid. At the breakfast table, they were distant and cool. It confused Liz, and she asked her parents if everything was okay.

All of her parents' emotion burst out at once. They told Liz she was irresponsible to stay out so late without calling. When her parents came down in anger, Liz felt the bonds created the night before quickly snap apart. It took most of the day and a talk with their pastor for Liz's parents to work through their emotions.

While they wanted to love their daughter unconditionally, Liz's insensitivity and disrespect, coupled with their fear and mistrust, pushed them beyond their limits. Their pastor encouraged them to be aware of their limits and to apologize for their reactions. He also urged them to talk with Liz about mature responsibility. Much to their surprise, their honesty reestablished trust and communication.

Liz's parents tapped the value of unconditional love, which is the safety net of grace. Grace says, "I love you, even when you let me down." It goes beyond human strength and comes from our relationship with Christ. Conditional love took over when circumstances pushed Liz's parents beyond their limits. The law says, "I love you if you conform and reject you when you don't." When Liz's parents returned to grace, they restored their relationship.

Black and White Isn't Always Right

Nature teaches us much about God. For example, did you know there are over 8,800 species of ants? Even the most casual observer must conclude that God is a creator who values variety and uniqueness.

The same is true of people. God made men and women in his image with unique personalities and characteristics. If everybody was the same, life might be easier, but it would be boring. The differences in people not only add variety, but they make life difficult and confusing, especially for the parents of a strong-willed child.

It is safe to say that a strong-willed child is harder to parent than one who conforms. It's not always pleasant to spend time with him. But it is wrong to conclude that a strong-willed child is "bad" while a conforming child is "good." Unfortunately, this is the black-and-white thinking that plagues unhealthy families. They label children based on feelings and emotional reactions. They overlook the fact that God created both types of children in his image with special redeeming qualities.

If you have both a strong-willed and a conforming child, you need to be realistic about their strengths and weaknesses, rather than resorting to black-and-white categorizations. For example, the strengths of the conforming child also have downsides. While the conforming child can be extremely cooperative in her dealings with people, she may be weak standing up to friends who challenge her Christian beliefs. Some parents discover that their conforming children grow up with less moral courage than their more difficult children. While they conform to the family's beliefs in their early years, they do not make them their own and abandon them in adolescence.

Conversely, have you ever considered the strengths of your strong-willed child? Does he have the ability to stand up to friends who could lead him in the wrong direction? Recognize that strength and praise him for it. Or if he resists your guidance, compliment him for his willpower. You might say, "George, you really are good at saying 'No' and being sure of what you want." This recognizes a potentially positive character trait when it's applied in the proper situation. It also shows respect and breaks old communication patterns.

Honesty is a commonly overlooked trait of the strong-willed child. Because the strong-willed child perceives himself outside the family system and its values, he sees the family dynamics clearly. And he isn't shy about saying what he thinks.

When Jennifer ran away from home, her neighbors and members of her church were baffled. Jennifer was one of five children of highly respected professional parents. From the outside, it seemed like Jennifer's home was the perfect American family. Even the social workers concluded this was a well-adjusted, happy home. They chalked up Jennifer's disappearance to rebellion.

When the authorities located Jennifer, she told the truth. She detailed the beatings administered by her father and showed her scars as proof. She revealed that her mother, brothers, and sisters received the same treatment. Everyone else in the family covered up the abuse out of fear. They were "loyal" to the family but ignored the sin within it. Only Jennifer spoke out and "betrayed" the system in an effort to protect herself and the rest of the family.

Labeling is unfair because it focuses on the strong-willed child's negative behavior, and makes that who they are. Labeling overlooks strengths in strong-willed children and weaknesses in conforming children. My grandmother used to say, "There is so much bad in the best of us, and so much good in the worst of us, that it isn't good for any of us to judge the rest of us." Draw on grace to recognize all sides of your children and see how God is at work in them.

Peeling Off the Labels

Despite our best intentions, it is easy to assign labels. When our strong-willed child's behavior doesn't meet our expectations, we get frustrated and angry. We ask ourselves, "What did I do to deserve a child like this? Am I receiving a curse from God for some past sin?" or we tell ourselves "My mom said I deserve a child like this after all I put her through!" When our child's behavior disappoints us repeatedly, we affix "the label." "John never cleans his room—he's lazy!" "Joanne is just stubborn. She never does what I ask!"

Sometimes the labels are implied. Most Christian parents know they should not be judgmental, critical, or demeaning. But their feelings seep into their relationships and they communicate the judgments of their hearts without words. They become distant, sigh heavily, frown, or use body language that shows disapproval. The message is, "We accept you when you act like us, but reject you when you don't."

Children are quick to perceive implied labeling. Your son, for example, may accuse you of favoritism by charging, "You like John better than me!" The statement may catch you off guard, and you may even deny it and assure him that you love all your children equally. But the best approach is to be honest and sensitive. If your child's behavior causes you to pull away so that he feels you are playing favorites, build a bridge of communication. You can say, "You know, Bobby, *sometimes* I do enjoy being with John a little more than you. But that's only when you argue and fight me. But Bobby, I really love you, even when I get frustrated with your behavior." This is loving, honest, and consistent with the situation. It relieves your frustration while your child sees that you expect cooperation and respect. It helps you avoid labels and protects you from being victimized by your child.

Communicating boundaries, or behavioral limits, is another way parents can avoid labeling. Without boundaries, loops and judgmental attitudes are more likely to occur. One mother, who previously allowed her son to call her names, set a boundary by saying, "If you call me a name, you'll get a time out and immediately go to your room." The judgments with which she labeled her son diminished when she established clear boundaries that protected her feelings.

There is always tension in families between the need to belong through conforming and the need to be an assertive individual. Ultimately, parents must recognize that having children who conform is not always good and having children who oppose is not always bad. The "good-bad" labels are untrue and unfair. More importantly, they cause parents to miss what God is doing for the family through the strong-willed child. Parents will always battle these feelings, but mature parents do not make decisions based on emotional judgments.

The religious system of Jesus' day incorrectly labeled him as a drunkard and blasphemer. The scribes and Pharisees were blind to Jesus' heart and his relationship with God because they focused on his nonconformity to their system. God in his grace became flesh to reveal their need and God's provision. But they missed their opportunity and failed to know him.

Our strong-willed children are certainly not God incarnate, but we can learn from them if we do not label and alienate them. When we know our strong-willed children better and understand their individual differences, we gain a better understanding of who we are and how we need to grow. Get to know your strong-willed child. Understand your role in his life and you will know yourself better. Seek to discover his heart and why God gave him to you. Find the things you enjoy about him and cultivate that enjoyment. Reveal yourself to him and require that he respect you. There is a good purpose for your strong-willed child if you avoid labeling him as "bad."

The Strong-Willed Child as Scapegoat

The Bible contains wonderful illustrations of God's sacrificial work on our behalf. One of them is the picture of the scapegoat. In Leviticus 16, God instructed Moses to select two goats without defect. He was to sacrifice one and send the other into the wilderness. The latter was the scapegoat who carried away the sins of Israel, just as Christ did thousands of years later.

Families have scapegoats, too, but they are far from innocent. Scapegoats are the family members who receive the brunt of the family's anger. They are "sacrificed" to cleanse the emotion that builds up in the family system.

THE SCAPEGOAT

Scapegoating is actually misplaced anger. When a person is angry with himself, his job, or other source of irritation, pressure and emotion build. If someone or something offends him, he can explode with anger inappropriate to the situation. The person who offends him becomes the scapegoat and receives the full force of his fury as a result of the circumstances.

Years ago my daughter Renee was crossing a major street on her way to school. The yellow warning lights were flashing and three lanes of cars stopped. One car in the far lane kept coming, however, and hit Renee in the crosswalk. It threw her in the air and she landed on her face. Instead of rushing to her aid or taking responsibility for the accident, the driver jumped out of the car, ran to my daughter, and yelled at her! Witnesses had to pull the driver away because of the anger she spewed. It was classic scapegoating: venting misplaced anger on the wrong person.

The strong-willed child in a family is usually the one who ends up being the scapegoat. When everyone is tense or tired, the strong-willed child's extreme behavior makes him the logical target for scapegoating. Scapegoating is dangerous and can escalate into hateful, vindictive relationships. To protect himself, the scapegoat may withdraw into his room or become angry and defiant, both of which irritate family members even more.

The strong-willed child who is the scapegoat may adopt a negative view of life or leave the house for self-protection. In severe situations, the scapegoat will conclude that life is unfair. He feels entitled to adopt a negative view of life and justifies his poor behavior.

One mother I counseled sided with her son for the first twelve years of his life when he came home from school and said that classmates were picking on him. "It was easy to believe him," she said, "because his father, teachers, and other kids were always on his case." But eventually she realized her son felt the "world owed him." He was impatient and always pointed out the flaws in others. He seldom gave credit where it was due and was selfish in relationships. It was only natural that others didn't want to associate with him. He was the scapegoat who found it hard to contribute. He was unaware of how his selfishness affected others, and he cut off relationships when others were selfish toward him.

While scapegoating is common, it requires unhealthy relationships to thrive. If scapegoating develops in your family, seek help from a pastor or counselor. If you are guilty of scapegoating, identify the real source of your anger and deal with it. One parent who grew up in a scapegoating family asked for his children's support. If he came home angry, he gave them permission to ask, "Dad, what are you angry about?" In this way, he focused on the family relationships by allowing his children to question his misplaced anger. In scapegoating families, each person needs to take responsibility for his own anger and deal with it constructively.

Belonging Begins with Yielding

Learning how to yield is extremely important for the strong-willed child who is the logical candidate to be the scapegoat. The strong-willed child views submission as losing. It is hard for him to believe that he can benefit by letting go of his will. But there are ways to help your strong-willed child see the fruit of conformity.

- Explain how people must learn to follow if they want to lead. Refer to the world of business and paying your dues to gain credibility.
- Use the scriptural concept of God's will to help your child understand the benefit of submission and surrender. The book of 1 Peter was written by a strong-willed man who learned to submit. It is an excellent book to read together.
- Ask questions that provoke your child to think about how submission helps him win in life.
- Look for teachable moments. Praise him when he successfully yields.
- Read the Serenity Prayer and discuss when it is wise to yield and when it is wise to stand.

God, grant me the serenity to accept the things I cannot change, the courage to change the things I can, and the wisdom to know the difference.

- Read biographies about great people who learned the value of surrender.
- Help him learn the value of appropriate nonconformity: doing things differently because he wants to, not because he needs to rebel. Praise him when he shows creativity in a task or explores an area of interest outside the family.

Keep in mind that the strong-willed child will find surrender to be a "questionable virtue." Be sure to share the benefits of surrender, like peace and rewards. Strong-willed children need to understand that God is good and that yielding to him is worthwhile. By the same token, your strong-willed child needs to know that he can trust you and that yielding to you will benefit him.

Another practical hint to remember is that the strong-willed child acts the way she feels. If her mood is positive, her behavior will be more appropriate. Changing her mood is often more helpful than attempting to change her behavior. Here are some suggestions for promoting a positive mood:

- Validate her feelings instead of resisting them. You can do this by treating them as normal. For example, you can say, "I'd be angry too, if I was left out of the game." Or you can use reflective listening: "So, you're angry that you didn't get to play in the game."

- Be affectionate and loving when she is upset and invite her to respond in kind. Give her a hug or reach out your hand to her.

- Every relationship has an emotional account. When you make deposits to the account by spending time with your child, you can draw from it without penalty. When the account is empty, your child will react negatively during difficult times. Invest in your relationship and maintain good will. Be conscious of the balance in the emotional account.

- Maintain a sense of humor. If you can produce laughter without sarcasm or disrespect, you can keep the mood positive.

- Spend time listening to your child in order to understand her behavior.

Grace Will Lead Your Home

You can lead your home by the law, but you'll only raise "law breakers." When the emphasis of your family is too focused on standards and values, you'll create a "good kid-bad kid" dynamic. If the emphasis on conforming is intense, your children may act out more extreme roles. They'll tend to live out the labels you assign. This invariably leads to alienation and scapegoating. And worst of all, you will miss what God wants to do for your family through your difficult child.

But grace will move your family toward God. When you apply grace to parenting, you place your dependence on God for the changes he wants to make in your family. You can relax because conformity and change aren't your responsibility alone. They reside in the hand of a sovereign God. You'll gain freedom to love your children and enjoy their individual differences. Grace enables you to accept the way things are and trust God for the way things should be. You can accept your children for who they are while you encourage them to take risks and mature. In the grace-based home, warmth and excitement are everyday experiences. Isn't it time to put grace to work in your family?

For Your Consideration

1. What emotions did Cain experience when God rejected his sacrifice? How did it affect his behavior?
2. Why is conformity in the family important?
3. What are the values, standards, and beliefs that are important in your family system? What bridges do you build that allow everyone to feel a sense of belonging and contribution?
4. What are the basic differences between law-oriented and grace-oriented families?
5. What areas of your family are law-oriented?
6. What positive traits does your opposing child possess? What weaknesses does your conforming child have?
7. How can you protect yourself from being victimized by your child? Think of an example.
8. What is scapegoating? How can you reverse it?
9. What does your strong-willed child need most in his life?

Skill Builders

Gaining Perspective. Switch positions with another member of the family. Talk about what it would be like to be in his or her position. How would you feel? Would you see things differently? Would you act differently?

Have everyone in the family change roles and play a board game together. Make it fun by having each member exaggerate the role he or she is playing, but keep it sensitive. After the game is over, talk about what it was like to be in another person's family role. You might also try switching roles in conflict to gain perspective and understanding.

Chapter Six

Moving Your Children Toward Maturity

And Jesus grew in wisdom and stature,
and in favor with God and men.

Luke 2:52

Let me introduce you to Charles.

Charles is forty-two and has never been on a date without his mother. Charles doesn't have much of a love life.

Charles isn't a confident man who attracts others. He apologizes for everything. He's sorry he speaks too softly. He's sorry he speaks too loudly. He's sorry he speaks at all.

There's a reason Charles is the way he is. It's his mother, Ruth. Ruth is not a confident person, either. She's afraid of the world and has not ventured out into it or mastered the skills that would allow her joy and success in life.

Ruth is an emotionally dependent woman who fell into reactive loops early on as a single parent. No one would believe it now, but Charles had been an angry and sarcastic child. He'd been stubborn and hard to handle. Raising Charles had required a lot of work on Ruth's part. But because she was so lonely, Ruth responded to Charles by smothering him with an overprotective love. He was all she had, and she criticized every woman who came into his life. When Charles expressed his independence, Ruth would often shame him for his lack of loyalty. "I've sacrificed my whole life for you," Ruth would chide. So Charles had given up fighting for emotional separation from his mother.

Becoming an Individual

There is a natural process created by God that allows a child to grow into a mature adult. It's called individuation, and it is the joyful process in which a child discovers who she is and how she differs from others. Through individuation, a child progresses steadily toward healthy, godly maturity. This is one of the most important processes in the mental, emotional, and spiritual health of a child.

The family plays a key role in this passage, either positive or negative. If families encourage growth, the child will become a healthy individual. He will express what he thinks, feels, and hopes without alienating others. He will be strong as a person and valuable in a group. To watch this process is a joy.

I'm a counselor whose world is relationships and communication. But my son, Christopher, is an excellent mathematician. His mother and I have concluded that his math skills came from a distant, unknown relative! By the time Chris was eight, we noticed that he enjoyed math. We gave him the opportunity to pick up extra math in summer school, and he was excited! In a self-paced fourth grade class, he worked through books for the fourth, fifth, and sixth grades, and tutored other students. He consistently tested in the top one percent of all math students and worked on advanced math concepts by the time he was a sophomore in high school. It was a joy for him to discover this great skill, and it was just as exciting for me to cultivate it and watch it grow. Christopher's acumen in mathematics was one component in his passage toward becoming his own person, and we had the thrill of assisting him.

But often the family hinders progress. A child begins life totally dependent on her mother. As she grows, she ventures out and recognizes that she

EMOTIONAL TAPE

is a separate person. At age two, she will show opposition for the first time as No! becomes her favorite word. As her growth continues, her mother is usually both elated and sad. She's elated because her child is growing. She's sad because her daughter is moving away from the special bond of infancy. But when a mother is overwhelmed by feelings of loss, she can overreact. If she feels like she is losing her daughter, she can initiate loops that keep her child from maturing into her own unique person.

God's desire is for every child to discover his or her special identity and nurture it to its full potential, just as Jesus did. When Jesus was twelve years old, his parents found him in the temple courts amazing those who listened to his insights. His parents were upset that Jesus wasn't with the caravan traveling back to their hometown. But Jesus made it clear that he understood what his life was to be about. He knew his mission was to be linked with his heavenly Father, and he was taking the first steps toward its fulfillment. He was becoming his own person. He was growing intellectually, physically, spiritually, and socially into the individual God wanted him to be. Luke described the process succinctly when he said, "And Jesus grew in wisdom and stature, and in favor with God and men" (Luke 2:52).

The Strong-Willed Child's Demand for Independence

Children possess an incredible drive to become individuals. The tactics they use to gain their freedom and identity can be extremely threatening to parents. Under normal circumstances, the process is difficult; for the parent of a strong-willed child, it is extreme. If intense loops develop, the damage that occurs in the parent-child relationship during adolescence can be difficult to repair.

Tim was the oldest of Janice's and Bill's four children. He was very strong-willed, and his parents felt defeated by him. When they confronted him, Tim had a way of punishing the whole family. He whined and complained until it was easier to avoid him and let him have his way. Tim had an unbelievable ability to make parenting seem futile. It took all the energy and self-discipline his parents could muster to stay emotionally disengaged. When they gave advice or made suggestions, Tim transformed it into a conflict.

One day Janice walked into the living room and saw the mess surrounding Tim. "If you're going to trash the living room, you'll have to clean it up before you go out," she said.

"I didn't do all this! Dad left papers on the floor, too. I'm not cleaning all this up!"

"Tim, I'm not going to argue with you. You may not leave this house until you clean this room."

Tim walked to a side table and picked up his mother's favorite vase. A cruel smile spread across his face and he dangled it between two fingers as if he was going to drop it on the table.

Janice braced herself and said, "If you break that vase, you'll replace it, Tim. You don't know how valuable it is."

Tim glared at his mom, trying to decide what to do. The expression on his face told Janice that he couldn't care less about the consequences he would face. She held her breath. Tim put down the vase and Janice left the room, shaking inside. The confrontation had not ended in disaster, but Janice knew from past experience how easily it could have.

After Janice composed herself, she returned to the room. "Tim, what we just went through hurt me," she said. "I don't want to have a relationship like this." Janice's honesty got through to Tim for once. They talked about what happened, and Tim apologized and even cleaned up the room.

It took hard work and growth for Janice not to react to Tim's defiance. She separated herself emotionally and allowed Tim the opportunity to make a responsible choice.

Making choices and foreseeing the consequences are difficult for strong-willed children. It is easier for them to define themselves by what they are against rather than what they believe in. They react against things, but have a difficult time building personal convictions that lead to a healthy identity.

The strong-willed child misuses power to get her way. Her tactics are simple: If parents do not give the freedom she demands, she punishes them. Parents and siblings are literally afraid to confront her for fear of her reaction.

This pattern is the opposite for the conforming child, who earns freedoms through responsibility and trust. A healthy family articulates its expectations, and the conforming child responds with obedience. The more she conforms, the more independence she gains. Responsibility earns independence.

In unhealthy families, communicating expectations isn't welcome. The strong-willed child reacts against his parents wishes and puts them on the defensive. It is hard for them to stand their ground without becoming angry or withdrawing in fear. During teenage years, some parents give up entirely. They don't expect their strong-willed child to cooperate, and so they stop making demands. They feel like powerless victims. Other parents confront and punish every opposing act or assertive behavior. One client told me his parents sent him to his room every Saturday night throughout high school. Neither position withdrawing or over-punishing empowers the strong-willed child to be responsible or independent. Finding the balance takes work.

Although Jesus opposed the hypocritical religious system of his day, he lived by his convictions. He knew his mission. He was able to be submissive. This is a challenge for strong-willed children. They tend to react against things in the absence of strong personal convictions. When opposing children learn to become individuals, they can learn new roles. They can conform when appropriate. They can contribute. And they can learn to initiate and flex according to the situation. It is up to parents to provide opportunities for strong-willed children to learn new roles and behaviors.

THE ENMESHED FAMILY

Short Circuits in the Individuation Process

The most important factor determining how well a child develops into an individual is his interaction with other family members. In positive circumstances, families can be a tremendous force in creating identity. If family members validate each other and avoid emotional reactions, a child has a better chance to be a healthy individual. He will learn to think, feel, and act for himself.

Unhealthy families, however, produce the opposite results. Often parents are not mature individuals in their own right. They react to their children and overly worry about them. The more anxiety they feel, the less freedom their children receive.

All children have strong drives to be individuals and not just extensions of their parents. Strong-willed children, however, demand their independence with a vengeance.

"It's my life. I have a right to do what I want!"

A claim like this often provokes parents to react and put restrictions on the strong-willed child, which of course only makes him angry and discouraged. It is difficult for the parent of a strong-willed child to refrain from short-circuiting the process of healthy individuation, because the child keeps inviting anger or anxiety.

One strong-willed teenager said, after bringing home a report card full of Ds and Fs, "Education isn't that important. I'll be out of this house in five years, so leave me alone." His parents got angry, grounded him "forever," and felt helpless and incapable of turning their son into a good student.

When parents react emotionally to their children, they reap negative, opposing responses. Some parents use guilt, fear, anger, or a sense of self-doubt to counter their children's attempts for independence. This invites children to rebel or withhold what the parents want. In either case, one emotional response produces another, and children find it difficult to be real and assertive. The more emotionally enmeshed parents and children are, the more reactive and fearful relationships become.

Don was a good man and well respected in his community. But he felt like he was losing control at home. When his children did not agree with him or questioned his values, he felt threatened. Instead of dealing with them rationally, he exploded and crushed their opinions through rage. In Don's mind, opposing opinions were equal to rebellion.

Not surprisingly, Don's children were afraid of him and cowered during times of conflict. What's worse, he wasn't aware of his fears and insecurities. He simply tried to control his family and did not realize the effects his anger had on his children.

When his oldest daughter, Shelley, became a teenager, she tried to assert her independence by questioning some of her parents' beliefs. But she was afraid to talk to her father, expecting him to come down hard on her. She retreated by talking only to her mother and bottling up her fear and sadness. She needed to grow, but growth meant courage.

One day Shelley and her father were arguing about the recent election and Don began to yell. Shelley's normal response was to withdraw to her room and feel hurt and resentful. But this time she took a different approach. For the first time in her life, Shelley looked her father squarely in the eyes and told him what she thought. She wasn't rebellious; she simply decided to be honest, whether he accepted her or not.

She shocked her father. Instead of becoming enraged, he saw a healthy assertiveness in his daughter. He found himself actually interested in what she had to say. For the next few minutes, he listened while Shelley mustered additional courage and poured out her thoughts and feelings. It was a landmark encounter in their relationship.

As children become individuals, they become emotionally mature. But children who do not receive permission to become individuals acquire negative emotional attributes. Dr. Murray Bowen, noted mental health authority, has studied children who fail to develop a sense of individual identity. Based on his work, I have witnessed the following characteristics of poorly individuated children.

They are easily frustrated and have a low tolerance for discomfort.

They waver between idolizing and crucifying others.

They have difficulty developing their own beliefs and convictions; other people tend to govern their thoughts.

They struggle between thoughts and feelings, with feelings usually dominating their lives.

They are not independent. Even if they do not live with their families, they still react emotionally to them or are dependent on them.

They have strong reactions to stress, and have a difficult time coping with their anger or anxiety.

They blame others rather than take personal responsibility for their lives.

While children need to take responsibility for their behavior, parents have a major task in learning how to trust God. One of the most difficult tasks parents face is learning to let go and allow their children to mature. Trusting God is a practical and effective solution. Parents who trust God for the welfare of their children will experience less anxiety than parents who fight to control their children's lives. And when children see their parents trust God, they learn how to trust him themselves. Emotional and spiritual maturity are the bountiful fruits of children who grow into healthy individuals.

Jesus and his mother experienced this challenge. Nowhere in Scripture does it say that Jesus ever rebelled against his family or their rules. But as he grew, he made it clear that his ultimate goals were to serve God. He was a man of great convictions and strong beliefs, characteristic of strongly individuated people. At the beginning of his ministry, Jesus' mother urged him to handle an embarrassing situation. At a wedding in Cana, the wine ran out and Mary prodded Jesus to replace it. In this account, Jesus clearly stated his ministry priorities. He asserted his identity while he met the need of the moment.

Later in his ministry he withstood the pressure of Peter. When Jesus announced to his disciples that the cross awaited him in Jerusalem, Peter reacted vehemently. He was afraid to lose Jesus. This would never happen to him as long as Peter was by his side. But Jesus wasn't swayed by Peter's fears. "Get behind me, Satan," he replied. Jesus asserted his own identity and withstood the pressure to compromise his convictions.

Two Strategies for Failure

Parents can hinder their children from becoming individuals if they rescue or react. These are opposing strategies that keep children stuck on dead center.

The Rescuer is the parent who assumes too much responsibility. She is overprotective and delivers her child from experiences that bring growth and maturity. Anxiety drives her, and she cannot bear to see her child work hard, take risks, or endure discomfort. In fact, when her child hurts, she suffers. The child with a rescuing parent doesn't learn to take responsibility because the Rescuer assumes it for him. If the child's homework is due, the rescuing parent gets nervous and takes charge. "Have you started your paper yet?" "You only have two days to finish. This is an important assignment." The parent may even do the paper to ease her own anxiety. The Rescuer will adapt to irresponsible, outrageous behavior without requiring change because change involves discomfort, something she doesn't want her child to endure.

One woman I counseled lacked vitality and enthusiasm for living. Her husband complained that she contributed little to their marriage and did not know how to endure everyday difficulties. But she was a woman whose mother was a Rescuer. "When I was growing up, my mother would relieve me of my responsibilities if they made me uncomfortable," she said. Now, years later, she was ill-equipped to live life and unable to accept suffering.

If the Rescuer doesn't allow her child to assume responsibility, a loop will develop in which the child will be continually dependent on the parent. The Rescuer needs to let go and step back from being overly responsible for the child. She can do this by developing outside interests and monitoring her emotions so she doesn't overreact. To do so, the Rescuer needs to identify the anxiety that drives her. Trusting her child to God is a logical first step that helps the Rescuer relax. If she learns how to trust God, and allows her child to face the normal struggles of life, she will help her child become a healthy individual.

At the opposite end of the spectrum is the Reactor. The parent who is a Reactor is underinvolved and distant. He is critical and demeans his child when behavior displeases him. Most of the interaction of a Reactor toward his child revolves around frustration and irritation: "Why isn't your room clean?" or "You never clean your room!" As a result, the Reactor undermines the confidence and courage of his child instead of empowering her emotionally. He discounts the child and says, "I'll clean it for you. You certainly can't do a decent job!" He is overly harsh and imposes stiff penalties for minor infractions. Or the Reactor simply ignores the child and distances himself to avoid frustration. All these behaviors hinder the child from becoming a responsible individual.

Anger is the emotion that drives the Reactor. It is not healthy anger that leads to honest confrontation and accountability, however. A responsible parent will use anger to move his child toward responsibility. The Reactor uses harsh, critical anger to force responsibility.

A Reactor needs more involvement with his child. He needs to invest one-on-one time in which he appreciates and bonds with the child. He needs to view his child positively and express confidence in her. If he reacts less, exercises more patience, and cooperates with his child, he will empower her to be responsible. The Reactor needs to define his expectations without condemnation. When he draws strength from God to connect with his child emotionally, he enables her to become a healthy individual.

Behind both of these failed strategies is the very real possibility that mothers and fathers are reacting to each other, with the child caught in the middle. One parent may be a Rescuer while the other is a Reactor. If they do not respect each other's strengths and recognize each other's weaknesses, they send conflicting, confusing signals to their child. Often, they may need marital counseling to balance the partnership.

Raising the Healthy Individual

What does the process of building a healthy, individuated child look like? One pastor described an incident in his own home that illustrates the point well.

Even though he was the pastor of an ultra-conservative church, his teenage daughter pressured him to see movies that made him and his wife uncomfortable. He was certain his congregation would be offended as well. He discussed the options with his wife and agreed on an approach that, although it made them uncomfortable, proved to be solid.

The pastor explained to his daughter that his conscience wouldn't let him see films like these, but he reinforced his love for her. He told her he didn't want movies or his role as a pastor to interfere with their relationship. When he explained his position and the motives behind it, he gave his daughter permission to make her own choices.

THE INDIVIDUATED FAMILY

While this may seem like a minor issue, it was a major cultural problem for the pastor and his church. What's more, his daughter chose to see the movies. It threatened her parents, but they stood by their decision.

After several months, their daughter changed her mind. She decided the movies weren't appropriate, and she told her parents she was through with her "life of sin."

This was a triumph of grace not only because of her ultimate decision, but because of the growth and individuation that occurred. The parents were healthy, strong individuals in their own right, and they sought the same for their daughter. Mom and Dad treated her as an individual, not simply an extension of themselves. They shared their concerns and feelings, but respected her thoughts and choices. The daughter knew her parents loved her. Above all, these parents trusted God and allowed him to work.

When the process of becoming an individual is short-circuited, the results are different. Even when parents are believers, their theology will not build healthy families if they're not strong individuals in their own right. Some years ago I administrated halfway houses for young men and women. One girl I met was a pastor's kid who underwent an abortion. She was totally alienated from her family and hated her father intensely.

As she grew up, she realized that her father was a tyrant. Even though he was a pastor, he was cold and domineering. He verbally and physically abused his children and controlled their lives. Independent choices were not tolerated, especially in moral areas. He did not respect their thoughts and feelings, and he treated his wife the same way. She was so dependent on him that she was incapable of standing up to him, even to defend her children. As a result, not one of the five children grew up walking with the Lord. Each one battled addictions with alcohol, drugs, or sex, and each one was unable to develop a stable life.

Even though this father was a believer, he did not trust his children to God. He forced everyone to think and act like he did. His children never learned to make choices that developed their own identities. They weren't individuals. They were merely extensions of their father, even in their rebellion. Their father was not a healthy, secure individual, either.

Proverbs highlights the difference in these two families. "Train a child in the way he should go, and when he is old he will not turn from it" (Prov. 22:6). The phrase "in the way he should go" is better translated "according to his way." The training of a child should be individually tailored, appropriate to the child's temperament and life situation. What are his strengths? What are his weaknesses? How does he learn best? What does he need to help him grow? This identifies the child as a separate person from the parent.

As parents thoughtfully consider the unique life of their child, they will not use a "one size fits all" method of training. They will establish an age-appropriate training with enough give-and-take to demonstrate respect.

I asked a pastor with three healthy, well-balanced adult children why his children turned out so well. He told me it wasn't as easy as it seemed. His middle child was very strong-willed, but his wife took special efforts to work with her in a unique fashion from the other children. Instead of fighting her daughter's differences, she valued and nurtured them so everyone could take pride in this special daughter. She accepted her and identified ways to make her feel like part of the family. In other words, she trained her according to her way, and reaped the benefits of discovery and growth.

When parents succeed in creating individuals, their children will:

- Cooperate with and care about others
- Maintain their relationships even in difficult times. They will avoid reacting negatively or distancing themselves from others
- Take care of their own needs without imposing on the welfare of others
- Base their behavior on personal thoughts, convictions, and beliefs rather than feelings
- Suffer discomfort to accomplish personal goals
- Define who they are without succumbing to the pressure of who everyone else thinks they should be
- Think realistically about their need for other people

Enabling your children to grow into individuals occurs only when you are growing too. The key is to ask yourself what areas of emotional and spiritual growth you need to pursue in order to help your child grow as well. Each parent starts from a level of individuation given by the family in which he or she was raised. No matter how healthy your home is, every parent has times when he or she reacts negatively, is disrespectful, or has difficulty trusting God. But as you overcome your weaknesses and give your children permission to grow, they will see that you expect them to become mature, healthy adults.

Finally, gauge each child's progress individually. Just as there are differences in strength between you and your spouse, your children will achieve different levels of emotional maturity. Refrain from comparing your children. Watch each one of them grow as you trust God in their lives.

Ready or Not, You're the Leader!

You may not feel like it, but you are a leader. You are appointed by God to lead your children. They watch you, take your lead, and learn from you. No one is more significant in your child's life than you. Dr. Haim Ginott, a noted psychologist, said a child cannot disagree with a parent's expectations of him. If your expectations are low, your child will probably live down to them. If your expectations are high, he will probably work to fulfill them.

Think Big is the story of Ben Carson. Ben and his brother grew up in a single parent household. His mother worked ten to fifteen hours a day to avoid welfare and raise her boys. Ben was not a good student and earned the dubious honor of being the slowest child in his fifth grade class. But that changed when Ben's mother decided to elevate her expectations of her sons.

She prayed about what she could do and put her plan into action. She cut the amount of TV her sons could watch to two programs a week. She required they read two books a week and write a report on them. But most importantly, she continually lifted their expectations of themselves. "Bennie," she would say, "you can be anything you want. Just ask God for help. God will help you if you'll help yourself by giving your best."*

After a few months, things began to change. One day Ben's teacher asked the class a question about a particular type of rock. No one could answer. Ben raised his hand, and the class began to snicker. But Ben not only identified the rock, he explained its formation. He amazed the class, impressed the teacher, and took his first steps as a superior student.

Ben's academic excellence grew and successfully led him through Yale and medical school at the University of Michigan. Doctor Ben Carson became the Director of Pediatric Neurosurgery at Johns Hopkins, the youngest man ever to head this prestigious department. Ben's mother was serious about her role, and he

---

*Ben Carson, M.D., with Cecil Murphy, *Think Big* (Grand Rapids: Zondervan, 1992), 29.

acknowledges the crucial part his mother played in lifting his expectations and turning his life around.

Parents can only give away what they have, but that is much more significant than they realize. When parents lead and positively affect the lives of their children, they provide valuable direction and values.

- They communicate expectations that bring out the best in their children and help them reach their potential.
- They give them responsibilities that empower them to grow. They hold them accountable to fulfill their responsibilities.
- They validate their children and make them feel important.
- They invest time, energy, and resources to give them experiences that provide growth.
- They are emotionally supportive but do not underestimate their children. They allow children to take risks without rescuing them.
- They believe in their children in realistic but challenging ways. They help them push through their doubts as they move from incompetence to competence.
- They focus on their own goals, well-being, and self-definition. In doing so, parents avoid focusing on their children to their own detriment. This gives children the freedom to define their own identity rather than be clones of their parents.
- They pray for their children.

Like healthy organizations, families function best under healthy leadership. The importance of a leader cannot be minimized. An organization is more apt to thrive when the leader is competent, self-assured, and emotionally healthy. A leaderless organization is anxious, especially in times of crisis. This is true for businesses, churches, teams, political parties—and families.

You may not feel like a great leader, but your contribution is immense. There are no insignificant people or unimportant contributions in God's kingdom. Families need parents who are leaders, who take their responsibilities seriously, and who trust God to help them fulfill their role.

Children with Special Needs

Some children have special needs that are beyond a parent's natural capabilities. There is no shame in admitting that your child needs specialized help, but first you must recognize the real problem.

Ron was a brilliant seven-year-old who read books well in advance of his years. But he was destructive and could not sit still in school. He wasn't learning, and his responses to his teachers' questions were consistently confused.

His frustrated parents brought him in for counseling, and I worked with the family on understanding and avoiding loops. This helped relationships at home, but Ron was still unmanageable at school. I sent Ron and his family to a doctor who specialized in problems like these, and he diagnosed Ron as ADD—Attention Deficit Disorder. He placed Ron on medication, and almost immediately Ron's ability to concentrate improved. He started to learn and told his mother that his head felt clearer and he "could hear better."

Prior to the diagnosis, Ron's parents struggled with guilt. They thought it was their fault that Ron was such a difficult child. His mother saw the angry glances of other parents who looked at her as if to say, "What's wrong with you? Can't you control your kid?" But Ron's problem was genetic and biochemical. All the parenting strategies in the world couldn't overcome this kind of problem. In Ron's case, as in many others, the best solution is the help of medical analysis and properly prescribed medications.

Children who have a difficult time paying attention and who are easily distracted may have Attention Deficit Disorder. Children who cannot sit still and are hyperactive may have Attention Deficit Hyperactivity Disorder. Both of these diagnoses are common in children today. ADD and ADHD have many characteristics that are similar to those of strong-willed children, so a trained, professional diagnosis is essential. Parents should see a counselor or psychiatrist to determine if one of these disorders is applicable to their child. I have found that approximately one-half of the children referred to my clinic by teachers for ADD or ADHD require medication. But medication isn't the only solution to special problems.

Some children who have difficulty learning or who constantly oppose require the creative solutions of special education. Sharon was one of my clients who was visually oriented and highly kinetic. She had limited auditory learning ability, and teaching her with traditional methods caused her to tune out and misbehave.

Her teacher finally transferred her to a special education class that employed music, motion, and visual tools as the main avenues for learning. Within one year, Sharon caught up to the rest of her class and excelled in her studies. As she became less frustrated, she began to cooperate. Sharon's unique learning requirements demanded special tools to grow.

Another family I counseled had an adopted son with whom they experienced tremendous power struggles. They dreamed that he would be a part of their family like their biological children, but he fought them continually.

One evening they saw a program on Fetal Alcohol Syndrome. They recalled that the birth mother of their son drank heavily during pregnancy, and they realized that his behavior was partly a result of alcohol abuse. While it relieved them to know the source of their son's difficulties, they felt guilty about the pressure and discipline they used that contributed to his misbehavior. Counseling enabled them to adapt their parenting style to fit his special background and needs.

The Road to Discovery

As you raise your children to be individuals, the process will be one of discovery and nurture. At times you will lead your children and at times you will follow. And you will make mistakes, just as your parents made mistakes raising you. But there are questions that can provide healthy parameters to help you develop children with a healthy sense of self:

- Who is this child God has given me?
- What is special or unique about him or her?
- How should I to respond to the differences in each of my children? What are my responsibilities in guiding and supporting them in their individual differences?

- Do I give responsibilities that help my children grow? Do I follow through to see that these responsibilities are completed?
- Is there anxiety in our family that makes it hard for my children to grow? Do I react to them in ways that hinder their growth? Do I challenge them to take risks, seek new experiences and work through their anxiety?

Perhaps the best way to view the process of growing healthy individuals is to look beyond your children. Raising healthy, individuated children equips them to raise healthy individuals in their future homes. The children you allow to mature today will provide grandchildren who have a legacy of emotional health on their side.

That's why your own Christian growth is so important. As you continue to grow in Christ and discover the person he wants you to be, you build a family atmosphere where your children are free to discover their own unique identities. In healthy homes, parents listen rather than react. They trust rather than worry. And they act from convictions, not just feelings. Every family will fail to some degree, but the investment in your child as an individual is an investment in his emotional well-being and in future generations.

For Your Consideration

1. How can being overly dependent keep you from taking care of yourself?
2. How do parents hinder their children from becoming individuals?
3. What are some of the fears you have as a parent that affect your children?
4. Where do you find the courage to work through your fears?
5. How does learning to trust God with specific fears or losses bring spiritual maturity?
6. What are some of the main differences in character and personality between you and your children?

7. How do your children demonstrate that they are maturing emotionally and spiritually? Refer to the list describing healthy individuals.

8. How do the strong-willed child and the conforming child differ in their quests for maturity?

9. Do you tend to be a Reactor or a Rescuer? In what ways?

10. In what ways are you a good leader for your children?

Skill Builders

Establish Power. Think of an area in your life in which you give away power. This would be in areas where you look to others to take responsibility for you, rather than looking to God or being responsible yourself. This is usually an area in which you feel incompetent, incapable, or lacking in knowledge.

Define what it would take to establish power in this area.

Example: Mary Jane, a single mom, felt she was a bad mother. As a result, she deferred responsibilities to her oldest son, John. This was easier for her than attempting to take the responsibility herself. It got to the point that her children answered to John before they answered to Mary Jane.

When she realized her overdependence on John, she asked God for wisdom and strength. She defined her role as a parent and assumed the responsibilities she had relinquished. Over time, she reassumed her role as mother.

Chapter Seven

Gaining Respect

She is clothed with strength and dignity;
she can laugh at the days to come.
Proverbs 31:25

It seemed like an easy question.

I asked a group of one hundred moms and dads how parents should gain the respect of children. "Do you gain respect by earning it—or by requiring it?"

One person responded immediately. "A child can't respect an abusive parent. It's impossible."

But another responded just as quickly. "The Bible says children are to honor their parents, and it doesn't say a thing about them deserving it."

This was not a theoretical issue. It was part of these parents daily lives, and they quickly divided along party lines. One group adamantly believed that parents should demand respect while the other argued that children give it when parents earn it.

The Bible says respect is foundational to the parent-child relationship. The fifth commandment says, "Honor your father and your mother, so that you may live long in the land the Lord your God is giving you" (Exodus 20:12). The biblical concept of "honor" means to give respect and value to another person. When parents are healthy and loving, it is easy for children to honor them. But it's a different story when they are irresponsible, unloving, or cruel.

In this sense, parents play a pivotal role in teaching their children to give honor. When parents value their children, they reap honor as a natural result. And when parents respectfully require children to treat them and others with respect, children learn to give it.

125

Children fulfill the fifth commandment when parents both model and expect respectful relationships.

For parents of the strong-willed child, however, the question of whether respect is required or earned may seem irrelevant. A parent may give respect and receive it back from a conforming child, but the strong-willed child is much less likely to reciprocate. Because she feels the world "owes her," she may expect kindness and respect without realizing she needs to return it. And because the strong-willed child is frequently reactive and defensive, she may lash out before she realizes her parents have offered her respect.

It is frustrating for any person to give and then receive little or nothing in return. And when it happens on a daily basis, as is usually the case with a strong-willed child, parents may give up and allow reactive loops to develop.

Loops are inevitable in families where parents are extremists. Some demand respect but do not give it. They coerce children to respect them. Their children may fear them, but they never love them. Other parents respect everybody else but themselves. They work hard to please their children, but they allow themselves to be taken advantage of. They simply don't expect and require respect.

Contrary to both of these extremes, healthy parents respect themselves and require the same from their children. They respect others and model this behavior in their homes. Balanced parents have practical know-how when it comes to building and expecting respect. This balance is absolutely essential for parents who are trying to establish mutual respect with a strong-willed child.

The Listening Ear

Respect grows when parents listen instead of just hear. There's a big difference between the two.

Hearing is allowing others to talk. Listening is understanding, empathizing with, and responding to what they say. In your adult relationships, you know when someone is really listening. That person understands your thoughts, your feelings, and your wants. You feel important because of the attentiveness you perceive. It is active listening, not passive hearing.

Your children are no different. They realize when you're tuned in to what they're saying.

Listening to your strong-willed child probably seems at times like hitting the "Play" button on a tape recorder. You hear the same whines, the same demands over and over. It's tempting to tune out or respond without really listening to what your child is saying. When you do respond, your child frequently acts as if he doesn't hear. To gain an audience with him requires tremendous patience and self-control. He is anxious to get his own point across, and his reactivity and defensiveness prevent him from listening in return.

Too often, give-and-take dialogue is missing between parent and child. Two monologues take its place. One person tries to get another's attention while the other defends himself, justifies himself, or simply tries to share his thoughts. It is a wonderful experience when parent and child speak to each other and make the "listening connection." But listening requires respect. It means receiving what the other person says. Do you allow give-and-take in conversations with your children? Who are the listeners and responders in your family? Which child do you have the most difficulty listening to?

The other fundamental of good listening is to acknowledge perspective. This means you value what your child says and attempt to understand his reality and his feelings. Your strong-willed child perceives things very differently from you. His perceptions may not always be realistic, but they are real to him. It is important that you do not discount his view just because you do not share it. And oftentimes his perspective is valid.

Roberta was a committed Christian who was raised in a dysfunctional home. She committed herself to be a better mother to her five children than her mother was to her. She worked hard to overcome her background. But her relationship with her children was difficult. She placed a high priority on principles and focused on what was important to her. Two of her children had been in trouble with the law, and Roberta was anxious to keep them out of further trouble.

But Roberta was a poor listener and wasn't receptive to what her children were saying. She exaggerated their offenses and they in response minimized her concerns. The children also did not listen to their mother, even though some of them were old enough to understand and listen with empathy.

During our counseling sessions, Roberta discounted her children's thoughts and feelings while she defended her own positions, sometimes to the point of yelling. In one session, two of her sons confronted her.

"Mom, we don't like it when you yell and won't let us talk!" her oldest son said.

"I'm a better mother than my mom ever was! You don't know how good you have it. You don't have anything to complain about!" she said defensively.

"How do all of you feel about what your mom just said?" I asked.

"Well," the oldest one said carefully, "it feels like she doesn't care about what we think. I tried to say what bugs us and she chewed us out!"

Roberta jumped in before I had a chance to ask her what she thought.

"They shouldn't feel that way!" she said. "I'm not doing anything wrong."

"Roberta, would you respond to what your son just shared? Do you know what he feels?"

"What they're thinking just isn't true!" she exclaimed. "I'm a good mother!"

"Roberta, do you think it's possible to be a good mother but still upset your children?"

Roberta didn't look at me, but acknowledged that my question might be true. "Yes," she said quietly.

Roberta's perspective was that she was a better mom than her mother, but wasn't getting the credit she deserved. Her children's reality was different. They felt hurt and disappointed when she yelled and didn't listen. Roberta and her children were not listening to each other, so they couldn't establish healthy, loving relationships. Even though Roberta loved her children, she discounted their thoughts and emotions. She did not respect their feelings, which alienated them even more. The intentions of her heart ("I want to be a good mother") were different than her children's experience ("She never listens"). Roberta needed to listen to her children and understand their perspectives in order to be the mother she wanted to be.

Parents and children will always have differing perspectives in the same situations. Only God is objective. Only he can see and understand everything clearly. But when parents allow their children to share their thoughts, feelings, and perceptions, they practice the essence of listening. This paves the way for children to respond or listen in return. When families listen, they demonstrate a practical application of respect.

Whom Do You Trust?

Trust requires respect. A child cannot trust you if she feels unimportant in your eyes.

One father wanted to teach his three-year-old that people could not be trusted. He stood him on the kitchen counter, opened his arms wide, and told him to "Jump!"

"Catch me, Daddy!" his excited son said as he leaped off the counter.

His father stepped back and his son hit the floor. After he picked him up, he had the "wonderful sensitivity" to explain the lesson: don't trust others; trust yourself. But who did this child learn not to trust? For the next several weeks, this little guy distanced himself from his father and avoided relationships with anybody in the family. When children can't trust, relationships die.

Christ demonstrated the need for trust. He proved that God is for us. He taught us that we can trust God because of his great love. Only a God who loves would give us his only son in order to prove that he values us as his creation. In essence, God earned our trust by his ultimate sacrifice.

That's why trust is central to Christianity. Trust in God builds relationship with him and creates loyalty toward him. We devote our lives to Christ because he sacrificed his life for us. We can endure tremendous hardships as long as we know we can trust him. God is our ally because we can trust him. The same holds true in families.

While every member of the family will value different things, healthy families will care about the things that are important to each member. Without this mutual caring, family members don't trust each other. They don't invest themselves in each other's lives. Trust needs to be cultivated by each family member in order build relationships.

Parents have more responsibility in this area simply because their maturity and age demand it. But children need to be responsible so that parents can trust them. Too often parents are emotional punching bags for children who are untrustworthy, irresponsible, incompetent, or lacking in character. Parents need to be trustworthy, but they need to expect the same from their children. Relationships require interdependence, each person doing his part to keep the relationship healthy.

Don wanted to trust his daughter. He believed that Christian fathers should love unconditionally, but he felt ripped off. He tried to trust Janet, but she opposed him and was irresponsible. When she said "yes," she really meant "no," and she rarely followed through on her commitments. Smoking made things more difficult. Each time Janet lied about her smoking, she killed a little more of her father's trust. The issue of trust became a loop in which Don and Janet reacted and justified their actions. They needed counseling.

I suggested they turn toward Christ and start thinking about each other. Janet seized the moment and asked her father if she could go out that night. Don was incredulous and refused.

And then, for some reason, he reconsidered. "All right, Janet. If you're home by eleven, you can go out."

Janet looked disappointed, and I realized she discounted the concession her father made. That night she stayed out until 3 A.M. It was the crushing blow to her furious father.

The next week I asked her why she disobeyed. "He doesn't care about what I want," she said coolly, "so I did what I pleased."

Janet was a trust-breaker. It was unrealistic to expect her father to continue cultivating trust if she didn't return the effort. Personal responsibility and interdependence are essential if families are going to trust each other. Children need to know their parents trust and respect them, but the same holds true for parents. What's more, parents and children need to be concerned for each other and demonstrate that concern in practical ways.

Trust and the Strong-Willed Child

A strong-willed child like Janet demands freedom and privileges in various ways, none of which earns a parent's trust. Sometimes she plays on the emotions of a sympathetic parent: "Mom, everybody gets to do what they want except me!" She complains, whines, gets angry or sad, but she never understands that privileges are earned. Sometimes these tactics work because parents vacillate between giving up or giving in.

Strong-willed children often lack dependability, consistency, responsiveness, and respect for others—precisely the traits that make up trustworthiness. A child who is opposing may earn his parents' trust one day, only to dash it to pieces the next day by being moody, unresponsive, and rebellious. His lack of understanding or care for how he affects others prevents him from earning trust.

One mother thought her daughter was hard of hearing. "She *must* be deaf because she ignores me until I scream!" She was teaching her daughter to respond only when she exploded. This mother needed to learn to ask once and then follow through on consequences to avoid feeling powerless and ignored. It takes more work up front but will keep her out of the danger zone where she yells from sheer frustration.

To break the loops that inhibit trust, parents need to change their behavior and allow God to work. Empowering a child to earn freedoms through responsibility is hard work that requires patience. This is especially difficult for the strong-willed child who feels he deserves special privileges. He thinks life is hard and unfair, and this attitude keeps him from earning freedom.

Rebecca pestered her parents for months to take piano lessons. Because she had a tendency to demand things and then give them up when she lost interest, her parents were reluctant to make the commitment. Finally they relented and found a teacher. Sure enough, after a few months, Rebecca began to balk about practicing her lesson. "I already did it," she would say, though her lack of progress belied her claim. Soon after-school practice time became a power struggle between Rebecca and her mother.

"You wanted to take lessons, Rebecca," her mother reminded her. "You *will* practice!"

"I hate piano!" Rebecca sobbed. "I can't do it—it's too hard!"

Rebecca and her mother were caught in an "anti-trust" loop. Even before allowing her to take piano lessons, Rebecca's parents didn't trust her to persevere. Rebecca, by lying about practicing, proved herself untrustworthy. Rebecca's parents broke the loop by showing their daughter that they trusted her to take responsibility for her practice time.

Rebecca's mother gave her a calendar on which Rebecca could record her practicing. In addition, she stopped reminding Rebecca to practice. "It's not my responsibility to make you practice, Rebecca," she told her. "I know you can do it. And Mrs. Jacobs will know if you haven't practiced enough." With her parents out of the "practicing" picture, Rebecca discovered the benefits of pleasing her teacher and, eventually, herself. She realized that taking responsibility for her practice time and proving herself trustworthy reaped valuable rewards: an enjoyment of music, the praise of her teacher and friends, and the respect of her parents.

A key verse for the strong-willed child is Proverbs 11:24: "One man gives freely, yet gains even more; another withholds unduly, but comes to poverty." The strong-willed child needs to learn that contributing can earn the freedom he desires.

On the other hand, there is a certain amount of trust parents should give automatically. They should let their children know they trust them and expect them to maintain it. If parents err in the area of trust, it should be on the side of too much trust, rather than too little.

Some parents believe the worst about their child. Avoid this thinking, even if the evidence leads you in that direction. This doesn't mean you're to be naive or deny obvious problems. It simply means you should believe the best while you perform non-reactive reality checks.

One father I counseled opened his mail and discovered a charge for a pornographic pay-per-view movie. He was furious and plotted how to punish his son. When his son arrived home from school, his father launched an interrogation complete with accusations.

"Dad!" his son pleaded, "Do you think I would order that kind of movie?"

His father felt stuck. He wanted to trust his son, but the movie was there on his bill. His son seemed sincere, but he had lied about lesser items in the past.

Dad backed off and did a little digging. The order for the movie came late at night when a friend of his son had slept over. After several phone calls, he determined that his son's buddy ordered the movie after everybody was asleep. He apologized to his son and learned that erring on the side of trust could have had a good reward.

Healthy families deal with trust judiciously. They teach their children to earn it and they give it to their children until they're proven wrong.

Allies

Trusting families have a team spirit. They encourage and pull for each other. They avoid alliances that make other family members the "villains."

Husband, wife, brothers, and sisters are allies who help solve problems. They sidestep loops, so no one wins at the expense of others. Parents are clearly in charge, but they consider the thoughts and feelings of their children. They respect each other enough to allow the family to meet needs when members ask for help or assert themselves. They cooperate from a spirit of goodwill.

This actually happens! But it occurs when mutual respect exists between parents and children. Adults and children honor each other through give-and-take relationships. These families don't even think about "winners" and "losers" because they know how to handle disappointment and solve problems together.

Other families aren't so successful. These families worry and feel powerless when they're under stress or when they cannot resolve conflict with each other. To cope, they form alliances within the family that make other family members the enemy.

Too often these families spend all their energy being disrespectful. They discount each other's thoughts and feelings. A parent may ask for help only to hear a teenage daughter say, "Why should I? None of my other friends have to do that kind of stuff!"

Sometimes a parent may think he understands the dynamics with his child but is actually out of touch. What's more, he doesn't ask the questions that could clarify the relationship. The child feels judged or misunderstood, and they attack each other. If they break their alliance, they will seek other allies to defend their positions. It may be a strong-willed child allied with strange, new friends versus Mom and Dad. It may be mother and son allied against a harsh father. Or it might be father and daughter versus an emotional mom.

Jerome spent twenty-six of his forty-two years in prison. When I met him, he told me about his life. His mother died when he was a boy. His father placed him, his brother, and his sister in an orphanage. His sister and brother were adopted, but no one showed any interest in Jerome. Left alone, something inside of him died. A numbness overtook him and he stopped caring about anything even his own life. When he outgrew the orphanage, he chose crime for his career. There was no one there for him. In his eyes, it was a logical choice for a man alone.

Jerome is an extreme example of what can happen when there is no ally. When people undergo stress, they seek allies for the loyalty and security they provide. Families are especially prone to rally together to meet a common threat.

But sometimes family members ally in the wrong direction. They talk *about* rather than *to* each other. "Do you know what Dad did again?" "Did you see Mom lose it at dinner?" Talking to a third person may vent angry feelings and tension, but it saps the energy needed to resolve the conflict. It makes the person being talked about the "outsider" and the "villain" instead of a member of the team.

But what can a family member do if she is afraid to talk with the person who upsets her? If the father, for example, is defensive or explodes in anger, it can be a terrifying experience. Or if a child intimidates his mother, she may withdraw and ally with her husband or a more compliant child.

The Cooper family filed into my office and immediately demonstrated their alliances: Parents and compliant son Todd sat together on the sofa, while strong-willed daughter Megan sat in a chair across the room. There was a chasm between them, both physically and emotionally. As the session began, Mr. and Mrs. Cooper and Todd talked about Megan as if she wasn't there. Megan's face grew hard and her body language defiant as her family pointed out her shortcomings. Megan invited their scorn and they unwittingly invited her rebellion. The Cooper alliance could talk with each other about Megan, but when they addressed her directly, the fireworks went off.

The most common alliances in struggling families are a parent and child against the other parent. Recall the Good Buy-Bad Guy parental loop I discussed in chapter two. The reactivity and disrespect between husband and wife can facilitate disrespect between parent and strong-willed child. When tensions arise between a nurturing parent and a tough-minded parent, they can lose respect for each other's roles and contributions. If Mom is too tough on the children, and Dad has to pick up the emotional pieces, she invites him to ally with the children. She becomes the outsider. The same thing can happen if Dad undermines her authority and allows the children to disobey. Mom becomes increasingly angry and feels alienated from her children and her husband. Mom, the "bad guy," needs to learn how to be responsible for her behavior to rid herself of her negative label. A strong-willed child can easily trigger additional conflicts between Mom and Dad.

Parents in the Good Guy-Bad Guy loop need to maintain their alliance by learning to listen to each other. They need to respect each other's strengths and trust God with each other's weaknesses. Their focus needs to be more on submitting to God than on the parenting style of the spouse.

Here are practical ways to avoid these broken alliances. Some of them may be difficult to implement without prayer and courage. You might even need a counselor's help if you cannot handle the situation on your own.

- Talk directly with the person who upsets you rather than to someone else. As you talk, validate his thoughts and feelings and ask for the same kind of treatment.
- If you feel overwhelmed and can't talk directly with the person, find someone to coach you. Identify a person who won't take sides or vilify the other person. Ask him to hold you accountable.
- If your child complains to you about your spouse, encourage him to talk directly with that parent. Encourage him to be assertive but respectful.
- If you see your spouse disciplining but not bonding with the children, encourage him to be receptive and responsive. Be on his side, but do not rescue or interfere.
- When you discipline, spend one-on-one time with your child to secure your bond with him. Build your own relationship with your child instead of relying on a more nurturing spouse.
- If your spouse is too soft with the children, be honest. Encourage her to hold the line. Don't react if she yields to the children. Provide space and pray that she becomes more balanced in her parenting.
- If you are a nurturing parent, learn to rely less on your spouse for discipline. Hold the line yourself. If your child is angry with you, learn to live with the emotional discomfort. Allow space for feelings to work themselves out.
- Above all, spend time with your spouse and strengthen your alliance. Talk about the kids and how you can work together

on their behalf. Have fun and do not let the children come between you.

Respect Versus Obedience

"He's a no-good loser!" Carl yelled. "He won't change. I know Sam, and he won't change!"

His family sat in silence. Everybody endured another blow-out counseling session between Sam and his father. To be sure, Sam was tough to parent. He was an angry young man with a strong will. He was a great disappointment to his father.

But Carl was difficult, too. He allowed Sam very few choices and reacted negatively to most of them. He demanded perfection, but of course, Sam couldn't meet his standards. Carl spent most of his energy calling Sam names or avoiding him.

I wanted them both to think about respect. If Carl gave Sam real choices, he could demonstrate respect toward his son. If Sam perceived that respect, he might make responsible choices. They could break their reactive, emotional loop.

I needed to press the issue, even if Carl was angry.

"Carl," I asked, "are there choices that Sam can make on his own?"

"Yes, but he has to obey!" Carl shouted.

"Are you able to make him obey you?"

"No!" he shouted.

"So, you're telling me that the way you're dealing with Sam just isn't working; is that correct?"

"Yes but he has to obey!"

"Do you want to force Sam to obey?"

"Now listen, if he's going to live in my house he has to obey!"

Carl was as furious with me as he was with Sam. (I felt like saying, "Well, you can't make me obey either, so there!")

"You know, Carl, I want Sam to obey, too," I said. "But force just won't cut it. There's another tool that's far more powerful."

Carl sat back in his chair and exhaled deeply. His anger exhausted him, and he crossed his arms as I explained the concept of respect.

"Sam doesn't think you respect him, Carl. And you think force is the only way to exert authority as a father. You don't feel good when Sam doesn't obey. You're hooked on getting his response."

Carl squinted in disapproval.

"But consider what respect can do. If you show Sam respect, I promise you that you'll gain the authority that you only dream of now."

"Give me a for instance," Carl said.

"For instance, you think that to be a parent you have to be one up on Sam. You think you have to be demanding and powerful," I said.

"When Sam disappoints you, you yell and lecture. You tell him what to do and you tell him what not to do. But have you ever told him how his actions affect you personally? Does Sam know what you really feel when the two of you argue and fight? Carl, if you communicate with Sam and give him real choices, you can show your son respect. And respect could change his life!"

That very week, Carl began a new approach with his son. He started by working through his emotional reactions to Sam's behavior privately before he approached his son. He took time-outs for himself, walked away from arguments, and prayed. He minimized the importance of what was bothering him. And he stressed to himself that Sam was responsible for his actions and God was ultimately responsible for Sam.

This produced a significant change in their relationship. Now Carl was able to communicate his concerns instead of rage about them. It also put him in a logical frame of mind to set acceptable boundaries for Sam's behavior. He established clear expectations and consequences, and dealt with Sam respectfully.

This new approach was enlightening for Carl. In the past, being more human and less "parental" never crossed his mind. But he was changing. Although it took about a year of counseling and practice before he could do all of this with consistency, Carl was a hard worker and stuck to his task. Sam saw the changes.

Sam realized that his father valued him. In fact, he saw that he loved him. Whether Sam obeyed or resisted, Carl attempted to deal with him consistently and respectfully. His father gave him real choices with real consequences. In one counseling session, Sam described his father's new approach.

"He told me, 'Sam, this is your choice. I can't make you do the right thing. But if you choose to go against the rules without talking to me first, here are the consequences.' He's never talked like that to me before," Sam said.

Sam used to get angry when his father refused to talk to him or yelled at his behavior. I shocked Sam when I told him that I would be angry, too. "I thought I was a bad person for having those feelings," he said with a tear in his eye. I explained that anger was normal in light of the unhealthy things that happened in his family. I validated his feelings of anger, but encouraged him to think about those feelings. It was a new idea for Sam to realize that he could feel one way but act differently, based on conviction.

Sam was an excellent learner. He recognized his anger without denial or shame, and began expressing his feelings and sin to God in powerful, emotional prayers. He wrote in his journal about his anger and found Bible verses that confronted his emotions. One of his favorites was "Do not take revenge, my friends, but leave room for God's wrath, for it is written: 'It is mine to avenge; I will repay'" (Rom. 12:19). Sam was learning to act less in anger and more in love and respect.

Carl and Sam are a tremendous success story for respect. They grew spiritually and expressed it in practical relationship. What Carl wanted was obedience. What he cultivated was mutual respect and cooperation.

The Nasties

Respect is a precious gift family members can give each other. Perhaps this "fractured fairy tale" will bring its value home.

Once upon a time, in a tiny village nestled at the foot of some beautiful mountains, lived the Nastie family. The mother's name was "DoanLemmieDown." She was a high-strung woman who was easily disappointed and had a quick temper. The father was named "Who-CaresIDon't," the most passive and easy-going man in the village. And the daughter was called "INeedYa," a beautiful girl who was starved for affection.

Strange names weren't the only odd thing about this village. Each night a unique phenomenon occurred. When people were kind and loving, the village radiated a warm glow that made the people feel happy and energetic. This phenomenon came from little glass spheres that the villagers carried in special pouches. When a villager gave a special glass ball to another villager who cared about him, it glowed with dazzling warmth. But if the villager ignored the gift, the ball faded into a cold, murky darkness, leaving the village cold and unfriendly. The villagers carefully protected their special glass spheres, because once they broke, they never gave light again. (This was the invention of a fairy who moonlighted at a counseling center, and who decided this village needed better social skills!)

The Nastie family cottage was cold and dark. When INeedYa gave a special glass ball to her father, he lost it. He didn't mean to, but he was busy and his thoughts were elsewhere. If her father found the time to share one of his glass spheres, INeedYa was ecstatic, and treasured the precious gift.

When INeedYa gave a glass ball to her mother, she had to be careful to do it at the right time. If DoanLemmieDown was angry, she threw the glass ball against the cottage wall. INeedYa watched in terror as the gift shattered and the life-giving glow faded into darkness. INeedYa's pouch was getting emptier all the time. When one of her spheres was lost or broken, something withered inside of her. Soon she didn't give her mother or father any more balls.

The cottage was darker than it had ever been before. WhoCaresIDon't and DoanLemmieDown began to demand that INeedYa share her spheres. She obeyed, but the Nastie family resented each other. When one of them finally shared a globe, the others neglected it. Sometimes INeedYa carelessly set a glowing ball on her dresser and let it roll off and break.

"What have you done?" WhoCaresIDon't would yell.

"It was an accident," INeedYa would casually say. "Besides, there's always more in your pouch."

As time went on, the Nasties broke more and more spheres. WhoCaresIDon't became increasingly angry, and DoanLemmieDown quit depending on her husband and daughter altogether.

One dark and dreary day, the Nasties ran out of spheres. As they sat glumly distant inside the dank cottage, a fairy appeared. The fairy told them they were going to reap what they had sown. Until a new supply of the special globes appeared, he sentenced the Nasties to live in the darkness of their relationships.

At first the Nasties blamed each other. They kept their distance until the darkness and cold overcame them. They snuggled together simply to survive. But an interesting thing began to happen. As they snuggled together, their suffering became a common enemy. They had to work together or freeze to death in their own cottage.

Smart fairy!

One cold night, the Nasties talked about their plight. They shared their hurts and resentments. They even began to forgive each other and promised to care for each other in the future. They made a vow that if they ever received new spheres, they would care for them day by day.

It was a joyful event when the fairy granted new globes to the Nastie cottage. They lived through the pain and were ready to start anew. Now each kind act and responsive gesture came with a glowing sphere. They built special stands to protect the balls from breaking and they called these stands "respect." They built walls inside the cottage to give each other space. Soon their rooms were full of brightly glowing balls. No one was afraid, and the cottage became a house that radiated light. Others came to the Nastie cottage and basked in the light of their home, especially families whose spheres were broken.

Perhaps the kindest act occurred when the fairy returned. So impressed was he that he erased the name on the cottage door. Instead of Nastie, he wrote the name Honorable. Then he changed the father's name to ICare. Mother's name became Dependable. And the daughter became Radiant.

The Path of Honor

One thing God detests is pretense. In the Old Testament book of Malachi, God characterized Israel's relationship with him as a farce. While they claimed to honor him, their actions proved the opposite. God admonished them to give him the honor he was due and quit pretending. His people needed the hard-edged truth in order to build a relationship of respect. Respect was paramount to God—and it's critical to families.

Is there respect in your home? Real respect is not just saying you respect your family. Nor is it merely promising to honor them. What's important is that your family actually experiences the fruit of respect: trust, loyalty, listening, and the commitment to work problems through.

I have never seen a healthy family in which members do not honor one another. And I've never seen an unhealthy family that is not disrespectful. Every family will fail at times, but the goal is to work toward respect. Honor one another. And be a person of honor who builds respect in your household.

For Your Consideration

1. In your family, is respect required, earned, or both?
2. How do you know when someone is listening to you?
3. Which relationships in your family are more likely to be two monologues instead of a dialogue? Why?
4. Which member of your family would say that you are a respectful person? Why?
5. Why is respecting others so critical to building trust?
6. What specific things does your strong-willed child do to break trust? How can he or she re-establish trust in those areas once it's broken?
7. Identify situations in your family where trust should be given. Identify situations where it should be earned.
8. Why is the reciprocal concept of giving and accepting respect so important in family relationships?
9. Who is the closest ally in your life? Is this alliance a beneficial one, or is it cutting out a member of your family?
10. What specific acts of respect could improve your family relationships?

Skill Builders

Give Choices. Is there an area where you have a hard time giving your child choices without reacting emotionally? Identify this area and make a commitment to give him choices without being punitive, reactive, or emotionally distant.

Example: James was angry that his son did not keep his room clean. He tried to be patient, but when the mess got to him, he either blew up in anger or distanced himself from his son. A friend encouraged him to give his son choices with consequences to head off these negative encounters.

Several weeks later, his son's room was in its usual state of chaos.

"Son, if you want privileges like playing after school, your room needs to be clean," he said. "It's your choice. If you choose to not clean your room, close the door and stay in your room while your friends are outside playing."

"That's not fair!" his son said. "I'll never get out to play."

"It's your choice, Son. You can go out and play if your room is clean."

"It's not fair!" his son exclaimed.

"You don't want to clean your room?" his father asked.

"I want to play no matter what my room looks like!"

"Well, Son, I may occasionally make an exception, but from here on out, your room must be clean before you play."

James sat back as his son became silent, thinking about what his father just said. After a few minutes, James began a conversation about something unrelated. The choices and consequences were set.

Chapter Eight

Achieving Emotional Stability

An anxious heart weighs a man down,
but a kind word cheers him up.
Proverbs 12:25

S ally couldn't sleep.

She felt like throwing up.

But that's the natural result of playing God and referee at the same time.

Sally's husband, Tim, and son, Richard, lived in their own head-strong world. They never thought about what they said; they simply blurted out whatever their emotions drove them to say. They lived amid a volatile network of feelings that triggered reactions they could not control. Pride, anger, rebellion, and revenge took their toll on family life. Sally tried to keep the peace. She stepped between her teenage son and middle-aged husband more than once to keep them from throwing punches.

But Sally couldn't carry the load forever. Her frayed emotions told her she was burning out. She came to counseling to find relief from a family that ran on emotions gone crazy. There seemed to be a force that was tearing her family apart.

An Ever-Present Power

Have you ever noticed how good days seem to fly by? And have you ever noticed how hard it is to get through the day when things *feel* wrong? Emotions are an ever-present force that colors our lives.

God created our emotions when he made man and woman, and we need to remind ourselves of his expert analysis: "and it was very good" (Gen. 1:31).

Your emotions and the emotions in the family system can reflect God's good creation. Love, joy, laughter, and encouragement all mirror emotions at their best. But reality shows us that we live in a fallen world where emotions can be harmful too.

Dad says something offensive and, without thinking, his son angrily defends himself. A teenage daughter's quest for independence stirs deep-seated emotions of loss in her mother, who responds by making major issues out of minor incidents. And the emotional volleyball played by an irresponsible son and overreactive mother poisons the relationships of everybody in the family.

Reactions like these make up the emotional systems inherent in every family. These emotional systems create forces that work like gravity, holding everybody by their power. When we overlook this aspect of life, we put our families in danger.

That's why we can't afford to take our emotions for granted. They govern our behavior, even when we do not realize it. In a fallen world we often forget that we can trust God, turn to him, and receive the wisdom we need to deal with our emotions.

You Shouldn't Feel That Way!

In some homes, it isn't safe to show emotions. Families respond to them with anger.

A child is sad, but the father mocks him. "You big baby! You're ten years old."

Mom is afraid, but her husband ridicules her. "That's a dumb way to feel! Nothing is going to happen."

"ANY OTHER FEELINGS ABOUT IT, SON?"

A child comes home from school happy, but his sister is full of sarcasm. "What are you so happy about, Smiley Face?"

Or a wife is angry because her husband overspent the checkbook, but she takes it out on her daughter. "Pick up your mess! You live like a pig!"

Immature families, especially when they are under stress, communicate that feelings are wrong. Family members react to each other, and the overriding message is, "You shouldn't feel what you're feeling."

You see this response from a tired, burdened mother. Her two-year-old begins to whine that she is hungry. "You're not hungry! You just ate!" she responds angrily. If Mom acknowledges her feelings—she is too tired to fix a snack—it would make her feel guilty. And even though she doesn't want to feel what she feels, she still does.

Dad walks in the door after suffering a hard day at work and humiliation by the boss. He steps on his daughter's doll and breaks off the head. His daughter's eyes fill with tears as she looks up at her father. "Oh, stop it! That was an old doll that should've been thrown out anyway!" he snaps. He doesn't want anything more to deal with.

In both of these encounters, Mom and Dad communicate that feelings aren't important. They're saying their children's feelings aren't valid, and they simply shouldn't feel that way. These are "don't feel" messages. But it's too late, because the emotion is already there.

This discounting of emotion happens in every family occasionally. When it occurs consistently, it is a clear sign the family is not healthy. The consequence of this is that the children fail to mature emotionally. When parents give a "don't feel" message, a child will feel guilty and ashamed of her emotions. She may even slip into a state of denial and cover up her feelings. She is ashamed of her thoughts and emotions, and she has no place to express them. Some children who live in homes like these turn to drugs. If they don't know how to develop good feelings that receive validation, they turn to chemicals to produce what they need.

Christian families add another twist to the issue of emotions when they overspiritualize. These families emphasize the spiritual to the point of denying other realities, such as the emotions.

Suppose a third grader comes home to a mother who over-spiritualizes. "I hate Sally!" the daughter says. Mom is afraid of emotions like these. She doesn't know how to discuss the problem so she denies that her daughter is struggling. She pretends that the feelings don't exist.

"Oh no, honey, you don't hate her," she says. "You love her—just like Jesus would want you to!"

Of course her daughter's hateful feelings aren't good, but denying their existence doesn't make them go away. This is overspiritualizing, and it does nothing to lead the child toward love and maturity.

Parents who overspiritualize to protect themselves from their children's emotional reactions can hinder their children's faith in God. In its ugliest form, parents "Bible-beat" a child to make him behave or feel differently. A parent who angrily reacts to a child's behavior and uses God to buttress his case may say, "God is going to get you for that!" It may make the parent feel peaceful, but it doesn't do a thing to help the child learn to process their feelings or look to God in faith.

Too Hot to Handle

Just like every other area of their lives, the conforming child and the opposing child handle emotions differently. If a conforming child has a bad day, a parent can sometimes tell him to change his attitude, and amazingly, he does it! It doesn't work that way for the strong-willed child. Anything can set her off. When she is miserable, she makes everybody else share her misery. If a parent tells her to change her attitude, she becomes even more negative. A strong-willed child invites more "don't feel" messages than the conforming child for obvious reasons.

First, she is usually less developed as an individual. This makes her less of her own person and more prone to react emotionally. Second, the strong-willed child feels emotions intensely and is more likely to express them, creating an emotional field in which whole families react. Parents usually find it is easier to distract her from a bad mood than it is to change it. Third, she tends to be the most angry or worried of the children in the family. She may even feel guilty about her anger but can't ask forgiveness. She is more content to blame the other person and bemoan how bad that person makes her feel. Dealing with the emotions of a strong-willed child requires validation, refusal to argue, and distraction.

James's twelfth year was a difficult one. His parents finalized their divorce and his father remarried. His mother treated him like the family scapegoat. And with his father's new relationship, he felt more alienated than ever. James's moods were black, and he seemed to suck the family into them. He made the whole family anxious. He badgered his father and sisters to get his way until they would have gladly sold him for a small profit. Even his stepmother was the target of name calling and abuse. The family sought counseling to deal with James's emotions.

The counselor worked hard to convince them that James's emotions were in need of validation. This meant James's father needed to identify with and understand his son's emotions while he held him accountable for appropriate behavior. Conflicts usually arose around James's stepmother.

"Come on, Dad! She's bossy and doesn't believe me when I tell her why I couldn't get my chores done. I can't win with her."

"Well, I'm sure that must be frustrating. I know you feel like she doesn't listen."

"She doesn't!"

"Nevertheless, I want you to treat her with respect and do what she asks."

"But Dad, I can't when she makes me angry!"

"Then take a little time and cool down," his father said. "When you're calm, come back and do what she asked you."

His father often tired of these encounters, but he stood his ground, and James learned to respond to his authority.

James's stepmother learned to refuse arguments, something that she had found impossible to do in the past. Key to this decision was her commitment to trust God in James's life, which made him less threatening to her. Her ability to distance herself from arguments frustrated James at first. He didn't like it when he tried to pick a fight and she wouldn't fight back.

Amid all the family changes, James's sisters had been his closest allies. But now James had alienated them with his negative moods and behavior. Counseling helped them take the "bad child" label off their brother and use humor to give him balance. Their counselor encouraged them to distract James with humor. It set a new mood and kept arguments from escalating.

One of James's favorite complaints was "Life sucks!" In the past, his sisters took him on toe-to-toe. "That's because you make it that way!" one of them would say. Or "Come on, James! It's your attitude that sucks!" Now they responded differently.

"Yeah, life sucks eggs—and sometimes they're rotten!"

This usually made everyone laugh and distracted James from his "complaint of the day."

Validating, refusing to argue, and distracting James from his bad mood all took pressure off the family dynamics. James was still a strong-willed child, but he began to respond to his family's love and matured as a result.

Getting a Handle on Emotions

To be sure, emotions can be difficult to deal with, especially when they come from a strong-willed child. Displays of emotion, be they good or bad, make some people very uncomfortable. But if families express emotions in healthy ways, they can learn to handle them.

First, family members need to be honest about their emotions and share them in responsible ways. One way to do this is to avoid statements of blame or projected anger. For example, if Dad walks into the garage and finds his tools scattered on the floor, he might attack the guilty child. "You *always* make a mess! You *never* clean up after yourself!" The trouble with this response is that it doesn't make Dad responsible for his own anger, and the child will probably defend himself instead of taking responsibility.

A better approach is to say, "I'm angry about the mess in the garage! You need to take care of the tools you left on the floor." In this case, Dad is honest about his emotions and the mess he found. He owns his own feelings. When a parent communicates his emotions clearly and honestly, his relationship with his son will be less reactive.

Projecting your anger on others and casting blame sparks conflicts. Owning your own emotions calms the situation.

This principle holds true for a variety of emotions. A fearful parent is sure to invite a conflict if she says, "I just know you're going to flunk! Go do your homework before you fail!" She will be honest and help her child if she says, "You know, I'm really nervous about this assignment you have. Please block out the time you need to finish it this evening." This mom is less likely to start an argument because she is honest about her feelings and realizes she is dependent on her child to relieve her anxiety.

Secondly, families need to receive each other's emotions and help each other process them in a godly way. This is the opposite of denial and validates the emotions and experiences each family member encounters.

In the case of the third grader who announced that she "hated Sally," Mom needed to hear her daughter out and help her work the emotions through. She could have said, "So, you had a tough day with Sally. Tell me what happened." This allows her daughter to share her anger, and Mom avoids condemning her for her feelings. It puts Mom in a position to help her daughter exercise forgiveness after she has released her anger.

Thirdly, parents need to learn how to validate feelings while they stick by their decisions. This isn't an easy task, especially when children exaggerate. The key is to understand the *emotion* in what's being said, and differentiate it from the *content* of what's being said. It looks like this:

Child: "Mom, you *never* let me wear jeans to school!" *(Exaggeration)*

Mom: "I let you wear jeans two weeks ago!" *(Statement of fact based on evaluation)*

Mom is working on content and the child is working on emotion. If the discussion continues to operate on two different levels, the argument will grow. If Mom heard the emotion, instead of just the content, she could have said, "It sounds like you're frustrated because I won't let you wear jeans today. I know that's hard for you, but I am not changing my mind." She validates her child's feelings, but holds to her decision.

Strong-willed children are much more difficult to validate. Emotions easily overwhelm them, and parents wish they could simply stop them from reacting so often. The reality is that some children function on a high level of feeling. They need more attention, not less. The challenge is to address their emotions in a way that helps them process their feelings and gain more freedom from them. Being honest about feelings, receiving them, and working them through, even if others aren't supportive, are essential to emotional maturity.

Fill 'er Up

It was hard to see why Sarah was struggling. It seemed like she had it all. She was an intelligent, good-looking girl with a great family. But three of her closest friends moved away. She fought to find a place in her youth group. And after working long hours to save for her senior trip, school officials canceled it. She was tired and glum. Her "emotional tank" was empty.

Children feed off their emotional tank: their store of good and bad emotions. When the tank is full, they feel good. When it's empty, they feel bad about themselves and are hard to motivate. They lose their vision for personal goals and relationships, and have difficulty seeing beyond themselves and their own experience. They take things personally, even if they're not intended that way. What's worse, once their tank is empty, it's difficult to fill it up again. The opposite is true when tanks are full, even for adults.

Emotional tanks get filled when we affirm, acknowledge, and appreciate each other. Families with full tanks allow members the room to express themselves. They relax and enjoy simple pleasures. They resolve conflicts, and treat each other with warmth and respect. Family members with full emotional tanks are able to pay attention to others, because others are paying attention to them. They feel a sense of belonging, both in the family and in God's universe.

When family members' tanks are full, they are less dependent on each other to feel good. They receive help when they're needy, and give it in return. The whole family strengthens itself. Parents with full emotional tanks have a special ability to withstand the darts their strong-willed children throw at them.

Three-year-old Johnny bounced around the living room while his mother entertained a friend. Every five minutes he interrupted his mother's conversation and demanded, "I want a popsicle!"

She tried to ignore him, but he persisted. Finally his mother said, "No, Johnny, and that's final!" A look of initial sadness turned into a scowl of anger as he crawled onto his mother's lap. He looked her squarely in the eyes and said, "If you don't give me a popsicle, then I won't be potty trained anymore!"

His three-year-old logic was amazing. If he didn't get what he wanted, Mom wasn't going to get what she wanted. Fortunately, Mom had a full emotional tank, and she laughed with her friend when Johnny left the room. Johnny's response could threaten and anger a parent with an empty tank.

When a family's tanks are empty, negative feelings rule behavior. Relationships deteriorate. Family members trade evil for evil ("If you withhold from me, I'll withhold from you"). They aren't faithful or kind as they focus on blaming each other. The major emphasis is on how each family member reacts to another's demands.

Stress, including the stress of dealing with a strong-willed child, can deplete a family's emotional tanks. When family members become locked in loops, they are unable to even think of each other, much less give support to each other. The more they react against each other, the more depleted their emotional tanks become.

Healthy Christian families draw life from God. He fills their tanks and enables each of them to love and maintain the emotional well-being of the whole family. They have a natural flow of give-and-take of which they are not even conscious.

Pay attention to your family's emotional tanks. What things do your children feel good about? What do they look forward to with anticipation? And what things drain their tanks of good feelings?

The Emotional Side of Discipline

Emotions go hand in hand with styles of discipline. As families grow emotionally and spiritually, they tend to move away from reactive, punitive punishment in favor of proactive, goal-oriented discipline. A spiritually and emotionally immature parent will punish based on the emotions of the moment.

This kind of reactive punishment is inconsistent. A mother will send an irritating child to his room on one occasion, but overlook the same offense later in the day because she is in a better mood. The motivation for her discipline is her emotions instead of what the child needs. Every parent will occasionally discipline out of emotion, but parents that are emotionally mature will seek consistency and focus on the child's growth.

Healthy discipline not only focuses on the needs of the child, but it protects parents. If a child forgets to do his chores, parents will follow through to help him take responsibility. Instead of exploding in anger, they act to help him fulfill his responsibility. This highlights the major difference between discipline and punishment.

Discipline is patient and goal-oriented, while punishment is punitive and motivated by anger or reactivity. The benefit of discipline is that emotions give way to purpose. It provides consistency that emotions-based punishment does not. The key to nonreactive discipline is the emotional maturity of the parents. Parents need to take stock of their ability to discipline. Every parent displays a mix of reactive and goal-oriented behaviors.

The less mature the parents, the more they worry and react. Worried parents will react to more situations than mature, relaxed parents. Their anxiety causes them to work harder because they identify more issues that need confronting. High-anxiety parents also overemphasize issues. Small conflicts are seen as big conflicts, and soon loops develop because no issue is exempt from conflict.

Jill transferred to a public high school after eight years of Christian school. It made her mother, Mary, nervous. The threats of rock music, gangs, drugs, and sex overwhelmed her. Of course, these are concerns every parent has, but Mary couldn't stop worrying. She focused all her energy on communicating these dangers to her daughter until Jill tuned her mother out.

One day, while Jill did her homework, her mother said, "I think some of your friends are into drugs."

"Yeah, sure, Mom," Jill mumbled as she kept on writing.

Jill's disrespectful response worried her mother, who pressed the issue further.

"Jill, I'm serious! Don't you care that your friends could ruin your life?"

"Mom, my friends don't even know what drugs look like!"

"Carrie does. Every time I see her she looks like she's on drugs to me."

"Mom!" Jill shouted, "Carrie is a straight A student! You can't do that and do drugs at the same time!"

"Yeah, well, she probably uses drugs to help her study," her mother said skeptically.

The two of them had created a loop where Mom maximized and Jill minimized. Mary dealt with her worry by maximizing the threats to Jill's life. She needed Jill to agree with her in order to make her feel secure. But Jill responded by minimizing the threats and trying to convince her mother that her fears were unfounded. Each of them needed to draw on God for healthy responses. Mary needed to trust God with her daughter's life and learn how to give her worries to him. And Jill needed to follow God's admonition to respect her parents. Both of them needed to listen to each other and respectfully talk about their feelings in order to develop a healthy relationship.

Other emotions like anger or guilt can make parents ineffective in discipline. In any of these situations, one emotional response triggers another, until parents and children lock up in emotional loops where no one makes responsible choices.

Anna Marie had come from an emotionally explosive family. Her mother was a screamer and her father an alcoholic. Anna Marie had become a Christian in her early twenties and felt she had escaped the craziness of her family. But her middle child, Jose, was very strong-willed, and Anna Marie found herself yelling at him just as her mother had done with her.

Jose did poorly at school, and about every two weeks Anna Marie received a call from the vice-principal. Her punishments at that time were punitive and reactive because she was so tired and frustrated with Jose. Through counseling, Anna Marie learned how to emotionally disengage and deal with her son in productive ways.

One day Jose came home and said, "The principal is going to call you again, but I didn't do anything." Anna Marie felt like wringing his neck but said instead, "Thanks for warning me." Jose looked surprised and walked away.

Sure enough, the vice-principal did call and said that Jose had kicked in a school door and broken the handle; the bill was one hundred and fifty dollars. Anna Marie didn't know whether to believe Jose's professed innocence or be furious with him for lying. She decided the best thing for Jose and herself was to make him take responsibility for the incident, whether he'd done it or not.

Anna Marie said to her son, "You will have to work this out with the vice-principal and figure out how to make things right." To her relief, Jose did as she asked.

When you see that your discipline is not working, stop and analyze the emotions that govern your behavior. When you identify harmful emotions, make a commitment to break these patterns. If you need help, see a Christian family counselor or join a support group.

Anna Marie started a support group for parents with strong-willed children. Through her support group, she found the encouragement to keep on disciplining Jose in effective ways, and she was able to help other parents as well.

Support groups can provide mutual sharing that will challenge you, while its members support you and supply the direction you need. As you grow spiritually and emotionally, you will become a proactive, mature parent, with a style of discipline that's driven by conviction, not emotions.

The Relaxed Parent

"Relaxed parent" isn't a contradiction in terms. In fact, a relaxed parent can make a huge difference in family life. When a parent lets go of worry, she can face family difficulties with a quiet confidence that things are going to be all right. She sees the big picture and reacts less to incidents and situations. In short, she has a deep trust in God, even amid difficulties.

One father expressed his trust in God after his son's arrest for shoplifting. "God isn't in heaven wringing his hands over our child's misbehavior," he said. Of course, he knew his son's behavior needed to be dealt with, but he knew God was still in control. He expressed confidence and strength in a potentially reactive and worrisome situation.

The relaxed parent is not the passive partner of an anxious, overly reactive spouse. He simply knows how to relax. He acts in non-reactive ways to establish order and reduce chaos. His character calms the family and reduces emotional outbursts.

It's important to realize that anyone can play this role in the family. During times of stress, the "relaxed parent" may be your pastor, a friend, or counselor. He is less vulnerable to the anxiety in the family and has a maturity that quiets fears. Relaxed parents model and teach the truth of Isaiah 30:15: "In quietness and trust is your strength."

Emotional and Spiritual Maturity

As children mature, their motivations change. They move beyond childish, emotional thinking. They don't need a reward to help them do what is right. Doing the right thing is reward enough, even though they still welcome praise or celebration of achievement.

Emotionally mature young adults don't need threats and negative consequences to act responsibly because they are responsible in character. They are confident and secure in knowing Christ and themselves. They take risks because they trust God and know that he will be there for them. And they know that trusting him means accepting the suffering, pain, and disappointment of life.

These young people appreciate their strengths and accept their weaknesses. They live beyond their feelings to achieve personal goals. They stay motivated, even in discouragement, because they know failure is as much a part of life as success. They don't have to impress anyone or express false modesty. They aren't self-absorbed like young children or adolescents, but care about others and understand their responsibilities to them. And they're free to focus on their own interests without guilt.

What motivates these young adults are the "want to's" of life, not just the "shoulds." This makes them less liable to be overly responsible people-pleasers. They listen to others without reacting, and assert themselves without antagonizing. They are realistic in their expectations of themselves and others. They move beyond the dependency of childhood, but know they are interdependent on others. They aren't prone to worry, and they flex with the normal stresses of life.

You may be wondering at this point if your strong-willed child will ever reach this level of maturity. The daily, even hourly, confrontations and emotional upheaval can easily shut out the light at the end of the tunnel. Raising a strong-willed child to maturity is without a doubt a long, difficult process. But it is one that can and will yield amazing results if you are willing to make the investments.

Emotionally healthy young adults don't wear a cape or have a big red "S" on their chests, but they function well. They rank at the top in emotional and spiritual maturity. And behind these healthy kids are families who made wise investments. They are families who helped each other grow emotionally and spiritually, and supplied the resources and leadership to move these children toward healthy lives in God. They encouraged their children to convert fear to courage, inadequacy to confidence, and vengeance to forgiveness.

Sheri Behr was a strong-willed middle child who hit her "rebellious peak" in adolescence. Even minor issues like going to church became major power struggles. Sheri would rather stay home and be sullen than be at church or school with friends. She frustrated her parents who labeled her as rebellious. But in actuality, Sheri was more worried than rebellious. During one of the family's counseling sessions, she told the truth.

"I'm scared," she said softly. "I feel like I'm out of place whenever I'm around people!"

"Can either of you remember what it felt like to be Sheri's age?" the counselor asked.

Sheri's mother nodded knowingly. "I was scared to death in high school. I really hoped you wouldn't be like me. I didn't want you to suffer the awkwardness I did."

But it was too late. Sheri was already like her, even though her mother did not know it.

"You know, Sheri, I'm still more comfortable around my tools than around people," her father said. "But I've come a long way."

"Then why do you treat me like a criminal for being afraid?" she pleaded.

"Sheri, honey, we didn't know you were afraid!" her father said. "You never told us!"

Both parents shared how they overcame their fears. They identified with Sheri's fear, but committed to help her grow.

In the months that followed, Sheri's parents followed through on their pledge. They pushed her to attend school activities despite her discomfort. They praised her for her courage and focused on her efforts instead of her fear. They urged her to act from a position of courage, and Sheri worked at being more outgoing with others. Sheri needed to change her beliefs in order to build her social skills, and she took up the challenge. Her parents invested in her, prayed for her, and put their trust in God, even when Sheri failed. They coaxed Sheri to come out of her shell, take risks, and grow. They encouraged her to transform her fears into confidence, and helped by replacing angry responses with supportive actions. Sheri's parents abandoned the failed strategy that simply told their daughter, "Don't feel that way!" Now they worked together to develop new skills and feelings in Sheri in which the whole family took pride. They relaxed and worked together.

As families mature, they develop an increasing sense of well-being, just like the Behrs did. They shame each other less and respond to each other more. They replace negative beliefs and emotions with positive goals. Even in difficult times, they accept intense emotions and work them through. They realize that God is both sovereign and redemptive.

Many people are far from achieving the level of emotional and spiritual maturity I described earlier. Their lives are full of ups and downs, and their character vacillates with each rise and fall. When family members are weak, the emotional problems are worse. Fear, mistrust, and anger control their lives, and they are numb to their emotions even though they are controlled by them. Fortunately, however, their lives don't have to stay that way.

According to Dr. Murray Bowen, most families live at a level of maturity governed by their relationships and thoughts. That's good news, because families can mature by strengthening relationships and patterns of thinking. By living out convictions, families can elevate actions above feelings. They can be proactive instead of reacting emotionally and unpredictably.

The Proactive Family

God intends for emotions to play a helpful role in family life. This means families are to validate each other's emotions and help process them. It means individuals are to react less and take responsibility for their feelings. It means families prohibit "don't feel" messages, and they listen to and respect each other. It means family members do not need to be ashamed of their feelings. All of these produce emotional health and spiritual maturity. As you move toward these exciting new levels of maturity, put these practical suggestions to work.

- Respect each other's limits.
- When someone in the family is reacting emotionally, give that person the space he needs. Separate yourself rather than react destructively. Don't go against your morals or your conscience.
- Validate and respect each other's feelings.
- Own your feelings. Don't blame them on others.
- Don't take responsibility for someone else's feelings. Think about how you affect them and take responsibility for your actions instead.
- Be realistic with yourself and others.
- Clarify family responsibilities.
- Trust God.
- Surrender to God things you cannot control.
- Don't be a victim. Don't let others victimize you.

- Make long-term decisions that will reduce tension in the family, even if they create more tension initially.

- Remember that your emotions are an important part of the family system. Healthy emotions contribute to your family's emotional and spiritual maturity.

For Your Consideration

1. How do emotions govern behavior?

2. In what areas of your family life are you most prone to sending "don't feel" messages?

3. Do you shame your children for their thoughts, feelings, or desires? How?

4. Think of several ways you can validate your strong-willed child's feelings, regardless of how strongly and frequently she expresses them.

5. How can you take responsibility for owning your feelings when you communicate them to your children?

6. Think of ways that you can help your strong-willed child process her feelings. Consider what you can do to change anger to forgiveness, fear to confidence, and sadness to gladness.

7. At what level is your child's emotional tank? At what level is your emotional tank?

8. What does emotional and spiritual maturity look like to you? How close are you to this goal?

Skill Builders

I-Messages. Practice using I-Messages for the next month. These are statements in which you own your own feelings instead of blaming others. When you communicate your feelings, you are less likely to invite negative reactions and more likely to help children become individuals.

Example: When the floor is dirty, a You-Message or blaming statement would be, "You *never* clean up the floor!" Sending an I-Message, however, would sound like this: "When the floor is dirty, I really feel frustrated. Would you please help?"

Learn to own your own feelings and not blame others when you communicate.

Chapter Nine

Developing Responsive Loops

A hot-tempered man stirs up dissension,
but a patient man calms a quarrel.

Proverbs 15:18

My wife and I had been struggling with our new son Tom's attitude for over a year, ever since he'd first come to live with us. Whenever we asked him to do something, he fought us, and it often seemed easier not to ask. But Lynn and I worked at not accepting invitations to reactive loops with Tom, and much of the time we succeeded. To invite him to contribute and be a part of the family took inspiration, as we learned one particularly jubilant week.

My staff had thrown me a birthday party and given me a sweatshirt that said, "I'm out of the loop." When I got home, I showed it to Lynn.

"I deserve one of those this week!" she said with a smile.

"Why?" I asked.

"Well, last night I asked Tom if he would do the pots and pans. He responded with a negative attitude: 'I always have to do everything around here.' I came back with, 'No, Tom, here is what you say: "Gee, Lynn, since you did four loads of laundry for me today and made me dinner, I'd be glad to do the pots and pans."' We both laughed and when Tom finished dinner, he got up and did the pots and pans."

Lynn had sidestepped a negative invitation to react and invited Tom to cooperate and be a part of the family. She was indeed "out of the loop"!

A Portrait of the Responsive Loop

So far, every time I've used the term "loop," the connotation has been negative. In the loops we've discussed, one person reacts to another in a negative fashion. This prompts a negative reaction in return, and a harmful loop begins. Each person works off the other with negative reactions that produce negative feelings.

But there is a positive loop, too: it is a reciprocal loop of positive responses and feelings. I call it the responsive loop. In the responsive loop, families still work off of each other, but they respond rather than react.

My son Chris was the number two seed on his junior high tennis team and content to stay there. "Hey, I'd like to be seeded number one," he said, "but I'd just get beat by the number one seed from the other school. If I stay number two, I can win. It's a safe place to be!"

Chris and I had fun teasing each other about being "number two," but I believed he could move into the top slot. "It's really up to you, Chris," I said. "If you want to be the best—and if you work hard to get it—you have a shot at being number one seed."

Chris tried hard but he lacked confidence. He battled ferociously but in vain during his practice matches against the number one seed on his own team. I let him talk out his frustration and did my best to encourage him. "It's tough to try and still fail," I said.

"It's not worth it, Dad! I feel like quitting when I try that hard and still can't win."

My goal was to listen to Chris until he could receive encouragement. "Keep fighting, Chris. You'll get there!" And slowly Chris responded. Feelings of encouragement replaced defeat.

Chris went undefeated in his second seed matches and lost only to Mr. Number One on his own team. It was appropriate that the city championships came down to these two. Chris knew he needed to play the match of his life. He began to believe that he could be the champ.

The fans couldn't have asked for better sets. Chris was up, then Number One was up. It seemed like the match went on for days. Finally Chris hit an impossible shot and won the match. He beat Number One and the city championship was his.

I'm convinced that the feedback Chris received at home played a part in bringing victory on the court. When he lost his practice matches, he was still a winner with me. I wasn't angry or discouraged with his performance. I didn't condemn him, and I didn't feel like a loser when he did not win. But that's what happens in some families.

In reactive homes, parents get angry with children who fail. Instead of encouraging them, parents condemn. Their self-image rests on the success of their children. When the children fail, the parents feel defeated, and they browbeat them to do better. Everybody feels bad and they lock themselves in angry, reactive loops. These are loops at their worst because they send messages that say, "You're nothing but a loser!"

But Chris and I had a different kind of loop: a responsive loop that built relationship and triumph. Responsive loops produce good feelings, quality efforts, responsibility, faith, and healthy self-esteem. They're loops that every family can pursue.

Responsive loops build positive moods like these and promote a healthy family atmosphere. They replace the strain that reactive loops produce. They help family members achieve their goals and build positive roles in the family. And best of all, they bring joy, elation, confidence, warmth, peace, and playfulness. What family wouldn't be thrilled to experience these traits coursing through their relationships?

Responsive loops are loops worth creating.

Inviting Responsive Loops

Parents can't force responsive loops, but they can invite them. They can act in ways that encourage and support positive responses from their children.

INITIATE POSITIVE INVITATIONS

When a parent invites a child to make a positive response and he accepts, it enables the parent to respond positively in return. The interaction looks like this: positive invitation, positive response, positive response, and conclusion with positive feelings. A responsive loop is completed. It doesn't matter who starts the loop. The important thing is for families to learn how to positively invite and positively respond to each other. It begins with simple acts.

It may be a mother who tells her son that she believes in him. He may hesitate to believe it at first, but he takes her encouragement seriously and gives a school assignment his best effort. When his mother sees his diligence to the task, she affirms and supports him all the more, and they both end up feeling good.

It may be a teenager who risks sharing something personal with his father. Instead of a token response, Dad drops what he's doing and listens intently. His father's sincere concern excites the teen, and he shares even more. Father and son have a rare time of closeness.

Or it may be a mother who gives her awkward daughter the opportunity to handle more responsibility. Her daughter responds to the positive challenge, works hard, and grows as a person. Her success makes her mother feel proud, and Mom shares her pride in her daughter's achievement.

All of these are positive responsive loops. Sometimes they develop quickly, and sometimes they develop over time. But all of them enable parents and children to build positive dynamics and good feelings.

While responsive loops sound simple, they are difficult for many families to achieve. A negative response at any point in the attempt to develop a responsive loop will short-circuit the process. Families with strong-willed children, especially those already caught up in negative loops, know this scenario well:

"You look nice today, sweetheart!" Mom says, attempting a positive interaction.

"Yeah, sure! I look terrible!" her grumpy daughter answers.

"No, you don't!" Mom responds.

"Oh, I do too! What do you want anyway?"

"Not a thing!" Mom exclaims. "Excuse me for caring!"

It's frustrating for parents to receive rejection to positive invitations. But continual invitations and respect demonstrate a willingness to invest in the relationship. If parents can be realistic about the responses they might receive, they can prepare themselves for rejection and sidestep reactive loops.

"You look nice today, sweetheart!"

"Yeah sure! I look terrible!"

"I see. Sounds like you're not in the mood for compliments today."

"I just want to be left alone."

"Well, then I'll leave you alone, hon."

"Hey, I'm sorry, Mom. I'm just a grump today."

"Well," Mom says playfully, "you're forgiven, Miss Grumpy!"

Perhaps nothing illustrates responsive loops better than "Mr. Sad Sack." This is an excellent example from *Liberated Parents, Liberated Children* by Adele Faber and Elaine Mazlish. It focuses on a single mother named Nell and her experience in a parenting support group led by the famed psychologist, Dr. Haim Ginott. The italics are my comments for emphasis.

> Nell's voice trailed off. Then she blurted out, "Dr. Ginott, I haven't been able to find one thing about my son that's praiseworthy."
>
> "And that troubles you," he said with concern.
>
> "Well, it's an awful thing never to be able to say anything nice to your own child. If anyone can use a little praise, it's Kenneth. He's so lacking in confidence; he doesn't think he can do anything well. I guess he sees himself as a kind of nobody. You know, a mediocre student, a weak athlete."
>
> "How do you see him?" asked Dr. Ginott.
>
> Nell thought for a moment. "Well, the truth is, he really isn't very capable. I know I should be more understanding, but sometimes I get so irritated with him. I watch him walking around the house with his shoulders drooping and that hangdog expression. It's as if he's deliberately trying to be a Mr. Sad Sack." *(Invitations to reactive loops)*
>
> "You mean it's almost as if he's assumed a role for himself and everything he does must be in character?"
>
> "That's right!" Nell exclaimed. "Even when something nice happens to him, he finds a way not to enjoy it."
>
> She frowned deeply. "Maybe he is playing out a role. But if that's true, then what does it mean? Does it mean he's stuck with it? Is this the way he's going to be when he grows up?"
>
> "It's possible," answered Dr. Ginott, "unless someone, at some time, sees him differently."
>
> Nell looked bewildered. "I'm not sure I understand you."
>
> "Nell, a child cannot disagree with his parents' true expectations. If our expectations are low, then we can be sure that our child's aspirations will follow suit. A parent who says, 'My child will never amount to much,' is likely to see his prophecy fulfilled." *(Outcome of negative beliefs and reactive loops)*
>
> "But, Dr. Ginott," Nell cried out, "you said before that a self-image had to be realistic as well as positive. It would be unrealistic for me to have high expectations for Kenneth.

The fact is, he doesn't do well in school. The fact is, he's not dependable. The fact is, he is careless."

"The question now," Dr. Ginott said, " is how can we help a child change from undependable to dependable, from a mediocre student to a capable student, from someone who won't amount to very much to someone who will count for something."

"The answer is at once both simple and complicated: We treat a child as if he already is what we would like him to become." *(Positive invitations)*

Nell looked baffled. "I still don't understand," she said. "Do you mean I should try to visualize the kind of person Kenneth could be, and then act as if he already were that way?" She shrugged helplessly. "But, I have no idea what he could be."

"Nell, here's how I see your son." Dr. Ginott spoke slowly. "I see Kenneth as a boy struggling to become a man." *(Invitation to help individuation process)*

Nell blinked for a moment, "Yes, but how could he ever . . ."

Dr. Ginott stopped her. "It's a difficult subject we've opened up. You may want to take some time to think about it."

Someone introduced another topic. After a brief discussion, Dr. Ginott consulted his appointment schedule. He told us that he was going on an extended lecture tour, and that it would be a month before we could meet again.

ONE MONTH LATER.

When the initial greetings were over, Dr. Ginott scanned our circle and fixed his eyes on Nell. "You have something to tell us," he said.

Nell smiled shyly. "Do you mean it shows?" She hesitated, as if in doubt over whether to go on. Then she spoke with great fervor. "You have no idea how the last session affected me. Dr. Ginott, I couldn't get your words out of my mind—that Kenneth was struggling to become a man. Every time I'd think about it, I'd start to cry. I don't know why. Maybe it was just the picture of this sad, young boy working against all odds to achieve his manhood. And there was no one on his side . . . not even his mother."

Nell swallowed in an effort to compose herself. Then she continued. "Suddenly I had an overpowering desire to help him. He had such an enormous job ahead. I wanted to give him every bit of support possible.

"The next day I was suffused with my new mood. All my exchanges with Kenneth—even the most ordinary remarks—took on a different tone. For example, in the morning he came rushing back to the house for his sandwich; not an uncommon occurrence. 'I forgot my lunch,' he apologized. Well, instead of reprimanding him, I found myself cheerfully saying, 'It seems to me, Kenneth, you remembered your lunch—and just in time!' *(Sidesteps a negative invitation and comes back with a positive response)*

"Then that same afternoon, after school, Kenneth asked for hot cocoa. Again I surprised myself. I suggested that he make it for himself this time, and that he make a cup for me, too. *(Positive invitation)*

"I think that really startled him. You see, I've never let him near the stove before because of his carelessness.

"'How do you make it?' he asked.

"'The directions are on the box,' I said, and then I left. *(Positive invitation that invites individuation and confidence)*

"Three minutes later, the unmistakable smell of scorched milk filled the house. I dashed into the kitchen and there stood Kenneth—his shirt, his pants, his shoes, all covered with boiled-over cocoa. He was a woeful sight.

"'Boy, am I dumb!' he groaned. 'I can't do anything right.' *(Negative invitation)*

"Dr. Ginott, at that moment I thought of your classic illustration; 'The milk spilled. We need a sponge,' and I smiled inside. I said to Kenneth, 'Oh, I see the cocoa boiled over. You didn't want that to happen, did you?' Then I handed him an old towel and we both went to work on the cleanup. *(Positive invitation that invites responsibility rather than gives punishment)*

"As Kenneth wiped up the mess, he mumbled, 'I don't know why I make so many mistakes.' *(Negative invitation or communication of emotion that could hook parent)*

"I commiserated with him. 'A mistake can be discouraging. It can really knock the starch out of you. Do you know what your father used to say to me when I'd get mad at myself for making an error?' He'd say, 'Look at it this way, Nell. A mistake can be a present. It can help you discover something you never knew before.' *(Validates feelings and gives invitation to work through feelings)*

"Kenneth turned that over in his mind awhile. Then he said half jokingly, 'Yeah, I discovered that when you're boiling milk, you'd better not have the flame too high.' *(Responsiveness)*

"I was so pleased to see his effort at humor, I tried to answer in kind. 'That's an astute observation, Dr. Pasteur.' *(Responsive loop)*

"Do you know, it was the nicest day we ever had together." *(Ends with good feelings)*

Dr. Ginott beamed. "The style is the substance; the mood is the message," he said. "What I'm hearing is a change in the entire quality of a relationship. Nell, I'm wondering if you're aware of how helpful you were to your son when he bemoaned all his mistakes. The more common response would have been to deny Kenneth's feelings: 'You don't really make so many mistakes. Actually, you're very smart. In fact, you're really a lot smarter than you think.' That kind of 'reassurance' would only have aroused his doubts and anxieties." *("Don't feel" message)*

"I also noticed that Kenneth was a little reluctant to accept your new image of him. Often it's easier for a child to cling to his old self-defeating ways because at least they're familiar to him." *(Question of responsiveness or receptivity to parent's invitations)*

Nell listened carefully. "Then that might explain the business with the money!" she exclaimed. "Maybe he was trying to prove that my new confidence in him was unfounded. You see, the very next day, I gave him a five-dollar bill and asked him to pick up a few groceries for me, something I had never done. Well, he lost the money before he even got to the store. *(Negative invitation)*

"I was terribly upset. It seemed so deliberate, his losing it. I thought, 'I've been living in a dream world. He'll never change. He's just as irresponsible as ever.' I was too angry to even talk to him that night. *(Emotional reaction without giving an invitation)*

"But the next morning I awoke feeling calmer. Somehow I knew that I mustn't lose faith—that without my faith in him he'd be lost. So I did something that may seem very foolish to you. I handed Kenneth another five-dollar bill and the same grocery list. *(Another positive invitation rather than the emotional reaction)*

"He was astonished. He said, 'You mean, you trust me? After what happened yesterday?' *(Responsiveness)*

"I said, 'That was yesterday. Today is today.'

"An hour later I was working at my desk in the bedroom when I heard a sound of something being pushed under the door. It was an envelope with change and a note." Nell fumbled for a piece of paper in her pocketbook. She unfolded it and read tremulously:

"Dear Mom and a half,

I got everything except the tomatoes. They were too soft.

Love,

Ken *(Responsiveness)*

"Did you hear what he called me? I'm not even sure I know what it means. And his signature! He's never referred to himself as 'Ken' before." *(Positive responsive loop and good feeling)**

Isn't this an exciting account? Nell learned how to create positive loops with her son, despite the past pain she suffered. Parents who cannot create a positive, responsive loop may have too much emotional pain and mistrust between them and their child. Reconciliation is needed first. Asking for forgiveness, entering into each other's pain without reacting or justifying, and rebuilding trust is necessary. Often this takes time and a willingness to give each other space. However, with most parents and children, just the refusal to react and giving positive invitations will help create a more positive relationship. "Above all, love each other deeply, because love covers over a multitude of sins" (1 Peter 4:8).

Leading Responsive Loops

Nell showed tremendous leadership. She stuck to her purpose and worked hard to empower Ken and not react to him. But this is extremely difficult when you have a strong-willed child who affects you negatively. For parents with children who constantly invite them to feel bad about their relationship and parenting skills, the task seems overwhelming. These parents feel emotions other parents never do. Their feelings will inevitably drive them to react negatively to their children. Parenting children like these is hard work. Failures are unavoidable, but this does not mean that success is unattainable.

Parenting is like any other job. In order to excel, parents must work toward a specific goal. This means parents must invest time, energy, and their very being in order to do the job well. When parents choose to build responsive loops, they're investing in life. Perhaps this choice is one of the main differences between healthy families and those who live with reactive loops. Healthy families invest in their children without getting trapped in reactivity. They consistently make positive invitations. It may be that they have more energy, a more stable home situation, or children that are less opposing. But the main characteristic of these families is the presence of positive, responsive loops. Eventually responsive loops become natural and require little maintenance. But for families trapped in reactive loops, it will require a significant amount of work and personal discipline, especially if their children are strong-willed.

Strong-willed children can be well entrenched in negative roles. They are prone to revert to old patterns of relating, even if parents move away from their previous negative roles. Some children even respond more harshly when parents sidestep negative invitations and initiate positive ones. These children do what they know best. Change for them is often a slow and difficult process. They can learn new patterns, but it requires strength and endurance on the part of parents.

That's why conviction and follow-through are essential for parents who want to build positive loops. Half-hearted attempts will usually fail. Without commitment, parents retreat to reactive behavior when their children do not follow their lead and counter their parents with negative reactions. A countermove is what Kenneth did when he lost the five dollars his mother gave him. It was as if he said to his mom, "You're supposed to be frustrated and irritated with me! Remember? I'm Mr. Sad Sack!" Kenneth didn't say this, but he communicated it well through his countermove. Parents who are not prepared for this will be slaves to the old dynamics.

Parents with vision don't let obstacles distract them. The countermoves of their strong-willed children, even if they are not intentional, do not deter them from building positive directions. When a child returns evil for good, strong parents will work their feelings through privately. When they resolve them, they are ready to invite another positive response. The process isn't easy. Often these parents have many internal struggles to work through as they invite responsive loops.

Georgia and her son, Troy, made great progress as they moved from reactive to responsive loops. Georgia learned how to sidestep negative responses and how to make positive invitations a more natural part of her relationship with Troy. They hadn't had a major argument in two weeks, and Georgia enjoyed the peace in the house, even though she was worried that it couldn't last. Nevertheless, the new relationship with Troy amazed her as she chatted with him on the sofa one Saturday evening.

But Sunday morning Troy woke up grumpy and irritable. He insulted Georgia for no apparent reason. He hurt her feelings and made her begin to doubt the growth in their relationship. But to Georgia's credit, she didn't give in and fall prey to her old, reactive patterns.

"I'm not going to stand for this treatment," she thought. "Troy's insults don't have anything to do with me; he needs to work it out on his own."

"Lord," Georgia prayed silently, "help me! I don't want to act the way I used to. I don't know what's going on, but I pray that you'll help me do the right thing!"

Armed with resolve and prayer, Georgia sat down with Troy, who was pouting in the family room.

"Troy, I don't know why you're so nasty this morning, but I expect you to treat me with respect."

"Yeah, right! Like you treat me with respect!"

"I know something is bothering you, Troy. You and I have really enjoyed each other lately. If you want to talk, I'm willing to listen. But if you don't, you can go to your room and work it out on your own. I'm not going to let you take your frustrations out on me!"

Georgia wasn't sure how Troy perceived her comments. She felt like she was compassionate but firm. She thought about all she'd learned over the past months, and it pleased her that she didn't react negatively to Troy's foul mood.

"You know, I don't give a rip how you feel!" Troy snapped. "And I couldn't care less about what you're willing to do! You're the pain, so why don't you go to your room!"

Georgia slapped Troy across the face.

"You brat!" she shouted. "Get to your room until I tell you to come out!"

Georgia slumped back in her chair as Troy stomped to his room. "What happened?" she asked herself. She thought she had the situation under control, but it fell apart. She felt defeated, but her resolve remained. After an hour of cooling down, she went to Troy's room.

"Troy, I want to apologize for slapping you. I really do ask your forgiveness. And you can come out of your room when you're ready to apologize for the way you talked to me."

With that, Georgia left to wait for what seemed an eternity. Troy did not come out. Georgia's anxiety rose, and it was all she could do to keep from running back to Troy's room. She wanted to yell at him for not taking responsibility for his sin like she did for hers. She talked to herself to keep from giving in to old patterns. "I can't do it all," she thought. "Troy has to do his part." She rehearsed what she knew about taking too much responsibility. She knew she kept Troy from being responsible when she acted for him. And she prayed for patience. It was more than an hour before Georgia heard Troy's voice.

"Mom, I was nasty this morning. I'm sorry," Troy said from the top of the stairway. "I was angry that you were paying so much attention to Sarah, but I was afraid to say anything."

"But Troy," Georgia said as she held out her hand, signaling for him to come downstairs, "Sarah needed me too. I didn't even know I ignored you."

Georgia and Troy sat on the sofa. They talked about their fight and their love for each other. They did not condemn, and they talked about how to avoid another conflict like this.

When I met with Georgia later in the week, we talked about her failure, but there was plenty of praise, too. She took leadership as a parent and confronted her feelings as well as confronting her son. She trusted God for positive results. Georgia did the right things and reaped positive results. I have found that in healthy families, about 60 to 70 percent of these kinds of encounters can end up in responsive loops when parents follow through diligently and sincerely. The key is to commit in advance to the hard work and perseverance they require.

The Loop That Builds Responsibility

Georgia and Troy restored their relationship. But what if Georgia had not made Troy take responsibility for his actions? What if only one person works to solve a family problem? What if the parent is the only one who cares? This can happen when a parent is overly responsible.

An overly responsible parent invites her child to be irresponsible. After all, if Mom does everything, why should her child worry about responsibility? And the irony is that an overly responsible parent still must endure the frustration of her child's irresponsibility. Her anger makes the situation worse. In order to build a responsive loop, parent and child need to solve the problem together.

Nathan was a constant frustration for his mother, Luanne. She felt like she did all the work in their relationship and in the home. When she asked for help or gave a command, Nathan simply said, "No."

Luanne was sure a counselor could help Nathan become respectful and responsible. Her counselor surprised her, however, when she focused extra time on Luanne.

"Do you ever ask Nathan to help you solve the problems you face?" her counselor asked.

"Not really. When Nathan disobeys, I discipline him for his irresponsibility. But ask him to solve a problem? What a waste of time!"

"And why is that?"

"Because he doesn't care! He doesn't want to help!"

"Luanne, it seems to me that what you believe about Nathan keeps you from inviting his help. You believe you're responsible for everything," the counselor said.

Luanne wasn't impressed.

"Look at it this way," her counselor said. "What if your husband said, 'Luanne, I don't care about the house. It's all yours to maintain.' Would you accept that?"

"Probably! I could never let it go undone," Luanne laughed.

"That's right," the counselor chuckled. "You probably would! That's why I've got an assignment for you."

The counselor told Luanne to work with Nathan in the division of household tasks. She told Luanne to let Nathan know she needed help, but to communicate the need as an invitation to participate. The counselor wanted responsive loops to replace negative reactions. Luanne prepped for her assignment and sat down with her son.

"Nathan, the house is getting to be too much for me. I need your help," Luanne began. "I'm going to give up some of the things I do, and I want to know which tasks you're willing to take over. I really need your help to solve this problem."

A stillness settled over the room. This was not Nathan's idea of fun. As they talked about what needed to be done, however, Nathan volunteered for several duties.

"Well, I guess my room could be my job," Nathan said.

"Fair enough," Luanne replied. "I won't nag you or remind you, because your room is now your job. "If it isn't clean, I won't do it for you. I'll expect you to keep it clean."

"But what if I can't get it done?" Nathan asked.

"Well, hon, if you don't get it done, it's still not my job. If it's dirty, I'll let you know how I feel. But I'll expect you to get it done anyway. And do you know why?"

Nathan shook his head.

"Because, Nathan, you are a responsible child. You can do it!"

And Nathan did. He became part of the solution rather than part of the problem. It didn't happen overnight; this was a process, not magic. When Luanne gave away responsibility, she invited responsive loops. She involved Nathan in a cooperative effort instead of trying to solve the problem alone. She believed in Nathan instead of reacting to him.

The Building Blocks of Responsive Loops

Studies reveal the average American parent spends between fourteen and twenty-four minutes a week individually with their children. Of that time, seventy percent is spent in discipline. If this is true, parents aren't investing enough non-discipline time to make deposits to their children's emotional accounts. Responsive loops require time.

The problem is compounded if parents have a strong-willed child. Not only does she require more discipline, but the family becomes "problem-centered." Healthy parts of relationships are ignored, making it tough for parents and child to enjoy each other and build responsive loops.

But being a parent who leads means taking initiative. It means laying the groundwork for positive invitations to healthy, godly relationships. There are several ways parents can lay this foundation.

Make Investments

What does it mean to invest in your children? It means making contributions toward their welfare and growth. Investments can be in the form of advice, financial help, love, time, or shared experiences. The list is limitless, and so are the rewards.

Here in Tucson, there are hundreds of high school kids who need stable homes. That's why we opened our house to Tom. When Tom first arrived, he saw adults as people who let him down. He felt justified in his anger, and he was defensive and difficult to be around. But over the past year, Tom's progress has been marvelous.

One day I praised Tom's progress to a friend, who responded with an excellent point. "Sure, there's been growth. But you didn't mention all the sacrifice and hardship that came before the victories." He was right. It was a difficult year. At times, Tom and my family were fed up with each other. But we committed to the investment and waited for the returns.

When you invest in your children, you sow seeds of responsiveness and love, and you overcome their feelings that they are justified in doing wrong. Investing can be risky, but failure to invest is disastrous.

Meet Needs

The needs of children, even compliant ones, are endless. They need attention, security, a sense of belonging, touch, affection, security, and stimulation to name just a few. Strong-willed children have their own perspectives, and what may meet the needs of a conforming child may make a strong-willed child uncomfortable. Public attention, physical affection, and attempts at humor are just a few of the responses that can backfire on a strong-willed child. Parents may feel even more discouraged when their strong-willed child accepts the parents' kindness ungraciously and unthankfully.

A parent who invests in her child sees an unmet need and seeks to meet it, regardless of the child's response. A bored child needs stimulation. A hurt child needs comfort. A lonely child needs attention. And a worried child needs assurance. A responsive parent meets real needs, and with time and experience, she will learn the most appropriate ways of responding to all of her children. When she does, she tells them that they are valuable and loved.

Enjoy Your Children

When a parent enjoys his children, he follows in the footsteps of God. God expressed delight in his own son when he spoke from heaven. "This is my Son, whom I love; with him I am well pleased" (Matt. 3:17).

If you see your children as just another duty, you'll harm them instead of affirm them. The key is time. Parents need to make time to relax and enjoy their children. Even the most simple activities tell kids they're special. Jaylon is my five-year-old with whom I share an important pastime. We catch lizards together! While this may seem small to you, it's important to Jaylon. I even make it into his bedtime prayers. Jaylon never ceases to move me when he prays, "And thanks, God, that Dad went lizard hunting with me today."

Play

When the goal is enjoying their children, parents make time to play. It's a sure winner to make children more responsive.

What form does play take in your home? Whether it's your sense of humor or your little one's cries to "wrestle!", play is the catalyst for enjoyment. In our household, our youngest child Nolan is the "Master Teacher of Play." He constantly entertains the whole family. He loves to be tickled. When he sets out to charm us, he brings smiles to everyone, from his grandparents to his five-year-old brother. Nolan makes us feel good, and we are a more responsive family because of his playful spirit.

Strong-willed children sometimes play too rough or are mean when they play. This can discourage parents from trying to enjoy their children. Setting limits is important to keep things from going too far. My son Jaylon often provokes reactions in play because he will not stop and respect the limits. A "time out" enforces the concept of limits for him.

Communicate Realistic Expectations

Children need the security of their parents' love, but they need to be challenged with realistic expectations too. When parents communicate a realistic expectation like, "I want you to do your homework," the child learns to take responsibility. Ultimately, he makes his parents' expectations his own. It's the process of making the "shoulds" of life into the "want to's" of life. It takes years for this process to occur, but parents who lay out realistic expectations move their children toward responsibility and adulthood.

The strong-willed child will often respond negatively out of sheer habit or the need to assert himself, but then go ahead and make good on the expectation anyway. If parents refuse to react or give up, they will see progress in their strong-willed child, although it will come more slowly and with more difficulty. Knowing this about your child will help you be more realistic in your expectations.

The delicate balance is to keep expectations in line. Children feel defeated by unrealistic expectations. They conclude they'll never be good enough to achieve. Realistic expectations demonstrate belief in children. They prove that parents know their children well enough to guide them in practical ways.

Know Your Child

Every child is unique and has differing needs and abilities. Getting to know your child enables you to make meaningful connections in your relationship together. It brings substance to your relationship.

Renee is my only daughter and my "social child." She cares about others and invests herself deeply in them. In my relationship with her, I've realized that spending time talking about personal things is critical to her. Casual conversations alone don't feed Renee's need for depth. This is an aspect of Renee that didn't come automatically. I learned it over the years and cultivated our relationship by spending deep, quality time.

If we assume that we know our children without taking time to discover their thoughts, feelings, and desires, we are presumptuous. We have not earned the right to be heard. But when we know our children, inside and out, our contributions are more likely to meet their needs and not be expressions of our own desires.

This is especially true of strong-willed teenagers. Parents need to spend less time leading and more time following during these years. If a parent is a good listener and asks good questions rather than focusing on "shoulds" and "oughts," he is more likely to form a lasting alliance with his child.

Believe in Your Child

When you believe in your child, you give him courage. You communicate confidence in his potential and faith in his relationship with God. Both of these equip him to face life emotionally and spiritually prepared.

Unfortunately, parents can have "negative belief" about their child. Their fear drives them to believe that he will do something wrong instead of believing he will do something right. Because they focus on this belief to the detriment of their child's character strengths, they almost guarantee that he will fulfill their expectation.

When parents believe in their child, they provide him a platform on which to stand during times of self-doubt and struggle. It isn't always easy to muster this belief, especially if your child affects you in a negative way. This is where faith in Christ raises you above your feelings and frees you from being dependent on your child's behavior.

When the apostle Paul looked at this question of faith and his perception of others, he said this: "So from now on we regard no one from a worldly point of view. Though we once regarded Christ in this way, we do so no longer. Therefore, if anyone is in Christ, he is a new creation; the old has gone, the new has come!" (2 Cor. 5:16–17).

Do you have a "new perspective" of your child? Do you invite her to assume new responsibilities, roles, and behaviors that substantiate your perspective? It can be great fun for the parent of a strong-willed child to believe the best of her, simply because the journey from her negative role to a new, positive one can be dramatic and exciting.

When you believe the best about your child, you provide the opportunity for her to fulfill your new, positive expectations.

Show your children you believe in them and watch them live up to it.

Allow Independence

Parents need to allow their children to grow in independence. This allows everyone in the family to have a healthy separation that promotes a healthy intimacy. There are practical ways to do this.

When a child says, "I don't know the answer to this homework question," Mom could give him the answer. She is helpful but he doesn't learn. A better approach is to teach him to think and take personal responsibility. Over the years, parents gain freedom when their children assume responsibility.

When children become more independent, families also experience true intimacy. Children who learn to think for themselves and be their own people aren't forced to be like everybody else in the family. They're individuals, not clones. When everyone is free to be honest, their responses are genuine, not wrung out of obligation. When families talk together, independent children can say "yes" or "no" without fearing an emotional backlash.

Likewise, parents who are confident in their children aren't obligated to rescue them. They aren't motivated by guilt to meet every need their children have. Their kids even learn to accept "no" from their parents without feeling frustrated, worried, or abandoned. All of this produces more emotional freedom for everybody. Responsive loops are more likely to occur, and the family atmosphere will improve.

In families with strong-willed children, independence is the "red flag." The process of allowing and building independence is complicated by the strong-willed child's relentless and unacceptable attempts to achieve it. Parents may be tempted either to withhold independence or give too much just to avoid conflict. But strong-willed children can develop a healthy independence if parents persevere.

Keep Short Accounts

You can encourage responsive loops by keeping short accounts with your children and not allowing bad feelings to build up. Keeping short accounts involves two prerequisites.

First, parents need to be confident in their children and expect them to be responsible for their emotions. Second, family members need to be willing to work their conflicts through without being defensive. This means that parents and children need to listen to and deal with the emotions that family members communicate. When a junior high daughter tells her mother, "You promised to pick me up at 4:30, and you weren't there," Mom needs to deal with her hurt and anger. She keeps the relationship clean when she says, "I'm sorry I let you down. Would you forgive me?" If the conflict is major and the hurt runs deep, it may take more than one conversation to empty the bad feelings.

Emotionally volatile children need extra help in learning to keep short accounts. Encourage your child to minimize his reactions to hurt and disappointment. Help him take responsibility for his anger and hurtful responses. Show him ways to help himself feel better without depending on others for help. Try role playing when your child is in a good mood: "What can you do if someone makes you angry and doesn't apologize? How can you feel good anyway?"

If you as a parent are having too many encounters that upset you, and you cannot achieve neutrality before the next blow-up, take time-outs. Calming and detaching yourself will keep the conflicts short, even if they do reoccur.

When parents and children keep short accounts, they empty themselves of anger, resentment, fear, and guilt. When the accounts are short, responsive loops are more likely to occur.

For Your Consideration

1. What is a responsive loop?
2. Have you invited a responsive loop lately? Think of how you did it.
3. Why is it difficult to create positive responsive loops with a strong-willed child?
4. Why is leadership required to create a responsive loop?
5. In what ways is a parent more goal-oriented when he or she invites responsive loops?
6. Identify five specific ways you can invite a responsive loop with your strong-willed child.
7. How can you invite your child to take responsibility instead of trying to force her to do so?
8. Have you ever sidestepped a negative loop? Think of an example and identify how you gave a positive invitation in its place.
9. Of the building blocks for responsive loops, which ones are you most successful at achieving?
10. Which building blocks do you have the most difficulty achieving?

Skill Builders

Invite Responsive Loops. Make a list of ways that you can invite your child into responsive loops. Initiate them in your relationship.

Make a commitment to sidestep negative invitations from your child and think about creative countermoves that invite responsive loops.

Example:

Child: I got a bad evaluation from the teacher today. If she was any good, I'd ace this class! *(Negative invitation)*

Parent: So she's good at preventing her students from learning?

Child: Well, she doesn't help me learn!

Parent: So what would help you learn and do well in her class? *(Positive invitation)*

Child: I don't know, maybe a tutor. *(Response)*

Parent: We could find a tutor for that class, but what about missed assignments?

Child: Yeah, I've missed some, but I'll finish them up.

Chapter Ten

A Firm Foundation

I must pay attention to my own peace of mind,
for unless I do I am useless to myself and to others.
I simply become so over-involved
that I have nothing left to give.

Esther de Wall

C an parents give up too much for their children? Are there sacrifices that simply aren't healthy?

Mary and Rick invested everything in their children. Their family was their first priority. Their children received quality time, even if it meant there was no time left for Rick and Mary. They were in the front row at soccer games, gymnastics meets, and other youth activities. Rick even decided to leave his job as a policeman in order to spend more time with his children. They seemed like the ideal Christian family, until their thirteen-year-old daughter, Denise, began to break the rules.

When they came for counseling, Rick, Mary, and Denise each had their own agenda. Each one knew what the other had to do in order to "fix" the situation. They came to me to solve it.

Rick was fed up with Denise's rebellion. "I want her to quit being so independent!" he demanded. As we talked, he alternated between simply being angry at Denise and attacking her to make her feel guilty. As I listened, it was obvious that minor issues were major hurts and disappointments to him.

His guilt trips hit Denise hard. She cried through most of our sessions but wasn't hesitant to share how trapped she felt. "Nobody has to go through the garbage I have to go through!" she charged. "I've got the strictest parents I know!"

187

Mary worried constantly. She was caught in the crossfire between Denise and her husband. She wanted Rick to back off and Denise to obey. Over time, stress took its toll on Mary. The conflict strained the marriage and dampened her sexual drive, which made Rick even madder. Inwardly he blamed Denise for the lack of intimacy in his marriage.

"Do you ever relax together?" I asked Rick and Mary.

"Relax!" Rick exclaimed. "How can we go out and relax? If we leave the house, Denise will cook up some new scheme to bend the rules!"

Everything in the family focused on Denise. She was "the problem" that kept the family off balance. All of their focus and all of their energy went toward her, but the intense pressure only made the situation worse. Nobody in the family had space of his or her own, including the other children.

The first thing I wanted this family to do was to find room to be individuals.

"Why don't you two go out on a date," I suggested. "Leave the kids at home and spend some time paying attention to each other. Don't even talk about the kids. As a matter of fact, don't even tell the kids about your evening. Make it your special night that only you know about."

Two weeks later they told me about their romantic interlude.

"We canceled it," Mary said. "Robert had a soccer match we didn't know about, so we went to that instead."

Rick and Mary couldn't let Robert down, even though he did not tell them about the game. Their marriage suffered another blow in favor of the children.

The ironic part of Rick's and Mary's family was the fruit of their sacrifice. Rick and Mary weren't taking care of themselves. Rick felt like a failure as a husband and a father. Mary overate and lost the figure that first attracted Rick. Most of all, their relationship with God hit the rocks. They quit reading the Bible and were numb to the concept of commitment. They were angry at God for allowing Denise to be such a problem, especially since they sacrificed so much.

"It's not fair," Rick said. "It just doesn't seem right that God would allow Denise to be so bad when I quit my job to be a better father! I had tremendous opportunities on the police force, but I've lost it all to take the job I've got."

I asked Rick whether he felt God owed him for his sacrifice.

"Hey, I did what I thought was right and best for my family! Doesn't that count for something?"

What counted, I explained, was owning his choices and accepting the consequences. I wanted Rick to see that his choice was fine, but the pressure he put on God and Denise was not. While disappointment is natural, Rick was dependent on Denise to conform in order for him to feel good. He needed to work through his disappointment independently of Denise's behavior. Mary had similar struggles.

"I've prayed that God would take all of this away," she said. "I just want Denise to be the good girl I once knew. But when I pray, it seems like heaven is made out of brass."

Mary could think of nothing but God's deliverance. Without change, she found no peace. It was inconceivable to her that God would help her *through* her suffering instead of wiping it away. Without that understanding, her anger and disappointment toward God increased.

Situations like Rick's and Mary's are especially difficult. Parents who convince themselves that the only way to find peace is through the conformity of the strong-willed child will find it hard to accept that they need to spend more time on themselves.

Of course, if a child cooperates, it is easier for parents to develop a life of their own. But parents like Mary and Rick need to learn how to relax and enjoy life without being dependent on the child to change.

Getting a Life

Christians are familiar with the teaching that tells them to live for God and serve others. But can Christians—especially Christian parents—lose perspective on what this means? Can they abandon healthy self-interest and neglect their own needs and identity? Is it possible that parents may give so much that they actually become selfish by demanding specific responses from their children? And in contrast, is there such a thing as a "healthy selfishness"?

Christ actually appears to model such a healthy self-ishness, a selfishness that had nothing to do with sin and every-thing to do with fulfilling his mission. At times, he left the needy multitudes in order to be alone, pray, and refresh himself. The most loving man who ever lived seemed distant at times to those who needed him.

In John 11, Mary and Martha sent for Jesus to heal their brother Lazarus. But Jesus purposely stayed away and allowed Lazarus to die. Even though Jesus raised him from the dead to prove he was "the resurrection and the life," Mary and Martha suffered the pain of their brother's death while Jesus disregarded their request. Jesus' compas-sion and tears at Lazarus's tomb displayed his love for this

SHAKY FOUNDATION

special friend and his family, but he did not act the way Mary and Martha wanted.

Jesus was a marvelous paradox. He acted independently of oth-ers but demonstrated tremendous compassion. He was a strong indi-vidual whom people saw as loving and kind. The Lord and Master of all was the suffering servant. He trusted God and lived the life that God marked out for him. He ministered with compassion, but the people he ministered to did not control his life. He was secure enough in God to act separately from Mary and Martha but love them at the same time. He had a life beyond those he touched.

Parents likewise need to find a life, security, and joy beyond their children. They need identities formed and established separately from the response of sons and daughters. This does not deny the need I've mentioned to invest in children richly. But it does mean that parents must not make their children the source of their identity and security. The balance is tricky.

It is natural for parents to overly involve themselves in their children simply because families are so important. The difficulty comes when overinvolvement makes parents dependent on certain responses in order for them to be secure and happy. When that occurs, it is parents who become childish. Some parents, like Rick and Mary, overly involve themselves to the point of neglecting their own needs. They may look as if they're living a sacrificial Christian life, but they may actually be selfish, looking for their identity needs to be met in their children. Security, meaning, purpose, challenge, and joy come from something greater than that. They come from God. When parents gain a broader, more balanced view of God, he enables them to relax and avoid anxious overinvolvement. As a parent's world becomes larger, he becomes healthier and more secure.

No one could argue that Carla was not a great mom. She invested in her children and empowered them to be successful. But while she invested in her children, she forgot about herself. She neglected her appearance and became overweight and frumpy. She did not consider the emotional and physical aspects of life that could make her well-balanced, and it showed. Even God took second place to her kids.

Carla's oldest child was everything she hoped he would be, but her second child, Lisa, was disrespectful and rude. She had a hard time controlling her volatile emotions. Lisa quickly alienated her friends and took her frustration out on her mother.

Because Carla's children were the center of her life, she had a hard time setting limits and boundaries on Lisa's behavior. She was afraid that taking a stand would alienate her and ruin her relationship, so sometimes she coddled Lisa. But without boundaries on Lisa's behavior, Carla also exploded in anger when Lisa was rude and insulting. Carla did not respect herself, so she could not help her daughter learn the concept of self-respect either. And because Lisa was her emotional security, Carla could not step back and constructively help her take responsibility for her life.

I warned Carla about the danger of her entanglement. She needed a life of her own in order to be a healthy parent. I counseled her to take care of herself physically and pursue outside interests. This wasn't easy for Carla to accept, however. She was afraid of change and failure, but after eight months she overcame her fears and stepped out. As she did, I cautioned her that her growth might be met with opposition.

Sure enough, Lisa was arrested for shoplifting soon after Carla started a class at the university. Carla thought about quitting and spending extra time with her daughter. She felt guilty and doubted that pursuing interests of her own was the right thing to do. Lisa tested her mother's resolve.

Carla stood her ground. She chose not to rescue Lisa, but put the responsibility for her actions squarely back on Lisa's shoulders. She finished her class and earned an A. Throughout the year that followed, she worked on her diet, appearance, and other activities that made her feel healthy. Her husband noticed the difference. "This is the attractive woman I fell in love with," he said. "She was 'lost' in the family for a while, but it's great to have her back!"

Carla found the proper balance between family and self. She learned how to care for others while she met her own needs, too. To protect herself from losing her identity in her children, she developed a special checklist that hung on her refrigerator:

1. Am I doing something that challenges me and causes me to grow as a person?
2. Am I doing things that help me to be healthy? Do I eat right, get enough rest, exercise, do a good job, seek out enjoyment, maintain multiple sources of security, work through bad feelings, and take responsibility for my life?
3. Am I taking risks and moving towards healthy goals?
4. Do I have a good support system?
5. Am I trusting God for his protection and provision? Am I waiting on him?
6. Am I being too dependent or passive?
7. Have I set boundaries that bring self-respect from others? Am I being respectful?

8. Am I paying attention to what makes me feel good or bad? Am I doing anything constructive about the signals I see?

9. Am I freeing myself from anxiety and invitations to reactive loops? Am I initiating responsive loops?

10. Am I parenting my children in a way that is supportive and that empowers my children to be more independent?

This ten-point list served to keep Carla on track as she became a healthy individual and a more balanced mother. It was a blueprint for getting a life of her own.

Moving Forward

Stepping back from overinvolvement in your children and becoming your own person can be scary. Once you make mature decisions, you also own the consequences for them—even the mistakes. That's why some parents avoid growth and allow themselves to live in the familiar safety of negative loops. It is easier to blame someone else for life's difficulties than own up to our own deficiencies. "My life would be okay if it wasn't for my child! He's the one who makes me a nervous wreck!" a parent may charge. It feels good to blame a child, but the real weakness may be the parent's insecurity and inadequacy. Even some of the Bible's great men found it easier to blame others rather than trust God and own up to their own failures.

One of the classic examples of this is found in 1 Samuel 15. God gave Saul instructions for attacking the Amalekites and completely destroying them. But Saul was afraid of his own people. They demanded the best spoils of war be spared, and Saul was too weak to do as God commanded and destroy everything. He wanted popularity more than he wanted to lead. To cover his sin and make up for his inadequacy, Saul attempted to justify his behavior through religious acts. He spared the sheep to sacrifice to God!

Samuel cut off Saul's phony argument. "Does the Lord delight in burnt offerings and sacrifices as much as in obeying the voice of the Lord? To obey is better than sacrifice, and to heed is better than the fat of rams" (1 Sam. 15:22).

Obeying God often means doing something you feel inadequate to do. It requires trust in God to achieve his will. Like Saul, some

Christian parents find it easier to make a "sacrifice." They would rather do something they can control than take risks and trust God. It may look good, just as Saul's sacrifice looked good, but it is compromise. For Carla, doing the right thing required taking risks. It took courage and faith that challenged her to the core of her being. The easy sacrifice would have been to quit school and forsake personal interests, but it would only have produced emotional dependency.

Moving ahead is walking the paths God wants you to walk. It is living according to God's call for you, not trying to change someone else's life as a cover-up for personal shortcomings. When parents are responsible for their own growth, they help their children learn responsibility as well.

When Calamity Strikes

Risk and growth are difficult when suffering and loss disrupt families. At times like these, growth is the last thing families think about. Amid their helplessness and discouragement, their focus turns to self-protection and safety.

Ironically, this is usually when the strong-willed child chooses to act the worst. In the middle of stress and loss, he becomes more than the family can handle, and families deal with him negatively. Some parents will make him the scapegoat and invite negative loops. Others will pursue unhealthy addictions like overeating, drinking too much, overspending, overworking, taking drugs, or indulging in improper sexual behavior. All of this—the negative loops and addictive behaviors—keeps the family emotionally enmeshed. Members do not grieve their losses, which makes it hard to rebuild unity after the crisis is over.

The Moss family weathered—and barely survived—such a time. After fifteen years in business, Donald filed bankruptcy and lost more than his firm. He lost his self-worth and became an alcoholic. It seemed like the only comfort he received was drinking and yelling at his teenage son, Randy. Mrs. Moss did everything she could think of to maintain peace. She comforted Randy and tried to soothe her husband's spirit. The family was broken, and no one had the strength to help rebuild it.

The Moss family demonstrated in a tragically real way what happens when families suffer loss. Just when they needed order, chaos reigned. Instead of grieving together, family members threatened and abused each other. Their grief was too much to bear individually, and they hurt each other instead of building each other up. Reactive loops replaced stability and comfort.

The Moss family remained unstable for several years. It wasn't until Randy entered a care shelter that Donald faced his drinking problem. It was a long, slow process of individual healing before they could function together as a family.

Families constantly change, but families who endure a major crisis are changed forever. They may regain stability, but it has a different character and feel than they previously experienced. God in his wisdom puts each family on a personal journey of experiences and events. He also equips them to face that journey. Too often families want a quick fix to the pressures that face them. What God desires for them is to honestly face their pain, grieve, work hard, take risks, and grow.

The urge to survive and rebuild is a spiritual one. In my practice, nothing has been more clear to me. Families with a healthy spiritual life can overcome incredible obstacles. One client told me about his mother who contracted cancer when he was nine years old. Though her disease was fatal, she asked God to allow her to live until she raised each of her children and they were on their own. She battled cancer for twelve more years, but she survived until the last of her children left home. God's grace fired her vision and protected her life to complete the task.

Psychologists identify two kinds of hope in people. One is passive hope, where individuals put their trust in a good God. The other is an active hope in which people do their best in their circumstances. Both of these are part of the faith in God and the rebuilding that families often require. The process takes time and faith, but fortunately, it rests on a sovereign God who helps families recover and identify with David in Psalm 30:11–12: "You turned my wailing into dancing; you removed my sackcloth and clothed me with joy, that my heart may sing to you and not be silent."

Letting Go and Moving On

There are times when the best thing parents can do for a rebellious older child is to focus on their own lives and, in a sense, "give up" on her. Sometimes this refocusing is the only thing that brings change.

One mother with a rebellious older son related how he brought her to the absolute end of herself. She suffered through his opposition and rebellion for years, but the end came when she loaned him her car and he sold it for drugs. When he returned home, he had the audacity to ask for money! She felt abused and resentful. "I'm going on with my life," she said. "There's nothing more I can do. He'll either come out of this or he won't, but I'm done!"

One man I counseled typified how letting go can be effective. He had been an alcoholic for over ten years and was a veteran bar fighter. He'd been shot twice and had over forty inches of scars from knife wounds. It wasn't until his parents backed off and left him in jail that he decided to change his life.

Another man told me about his life of car theft that began at the age of twelve and lasted until he was eighteen. He told me the only thing that broke his behavior was when his mother stopped bailing him out of jail.

Parents work hard to be loyal to their children, sometimes to the point of doing too much for them. They create loops where they overfunction and their children underfunction. Eventually they reach a breaking point—and that is legitimate. Parents in this situation don't need to feel guilty about letting their children go. If they

allow their children to stand on their own and reap consequences, change may come.

Too often, however, parents who release their children do not stick to their decision. Once they feel better about being at a distance, they reestablish an unhealthy relationship when they see their children continuing to struggle. It may make parents feel better to become reinvolved, but it keeps them subject to the tyranny of their children.

When Parents Grow Up

When you as a parent become a healthy individual, you learn what it means to grow up. You learn that sometimes you will stand alone. When you move away from loops and build a life of your own, you disrupt the status quo of unhealthy relationships. Not everybody likes that. Children, family, and friends may disagree with your new style of parenting.

Your child may say, "You're mean! I want my old mom back!" Your neighbor may question you: "Doesn't it seem a little cruel to let her cry?" A whole host of questioning and blaming statements await parents who pursue new directions. It's not easy to stand under such pressure.

Children aren't afraid to attack your methods in order to reestablish the old roles from which you moved away. "You're selfish! If it wasn't for you, I'd be happy!" What they secretly desire is to have you be the parent they want, not the person you are.

Most of the pressures you will face revolve around fear. Most often, parents are afraid their children or family will reject them. One mother's son constantly threatened to run away from home unless she did what he wanted. She knew better than to give in, but she was afraid to draw the line. She was afraid her son would make good on his threat, and she could not bear the thought of her mother's anger if she learned her grandson was gone.

It is difficult not to cave in under pressure like that. Only when parents grow as individuals, develop strong convictions and a personal walk with God, will they be able to survive this emotional quagmire.

One helpful thing parents can do is to think through their convictions and define them for their children. This will help them clarify who they are, and it will help children understand how their parents want relationships to work. It is especially helpful because it allows parents to exercise authority with sincerity and sensitivity. They sidestep reactive loops and allow their children to own their own disappointment at their parents' decisions. Knowing who you are helps you to be assertive and sensitive at the same time.

Don't confuse assertiveness with anger, however. Parents who confuse the two tend to be reactive instead of assertive. While anger can be positive, it can also be disrespectful and cause alienation. Parents who angrily declare that they're in control may be exercising nothing more than a rebellious response to fear that is out of control. It destroys their credibility.

Consider the teenager who angrily declares, "I'm sixteen, and I demand to be treated like an adult!" Many parents may become angry or afraid of such a selfish approach. The most likely response the teen will receive is, "Then act like an adult and we'll treat you like one!" But what if the teen thinks her position through? How much more receptive will her parents be if she says, "Mom, I'm sixteen years old. It really bothers me when you treat me like a child. Would you be willing to treat me like a teenager?" Chances are most parents will be more willing to work toward intimacy when presented with an approach like this.

Parents need to use the same approach. Assertiveness on the part of parents clarifies their identity but does not sacrifice family closeness. It allows family members to talk, express their feelings, and ask questions. It promotes respect and a willingness to listen, as well as making expectations clear.

There's nothing selfish about being assertive. All that's required is for parents to think through the kind of parents they are and want to be, and express those beliefs clearly and respectfully. It's all part of growing up as parents, and it enables moms and dads to respond to their children while they exercise leadership over them.

Looking at Yourself

The primary shift that must take place in a family with a strong-willed child is a change in focus. It is easy for the strong-willed child to be the negative nucleus of the family. Parents need instead to allow God to be the positive, central focus.

This is a difficult task. The family is a system in which members affect each other. A strong-willed child draws everyone's attention and energy by his behavior. Turning to God in trust means that parents must allow God to come between themselves and their child. They need to develop a deeper walk with God and separate themselves emotionally from the worry and intensity surrounding their strong-willed child. They need to disengage and deal with their own emotions and issues. If even one parent in the household begins to break free and grow, the family will benefit, despite resistance by other family members.

Have you found that your attempts to bring your opposing son or daughter in line with your family system just aren't working? In the introduction to this book, I stated my belief that the difficulties of raising a strong-willed child must be addressed within the family as a whole. A step-by-step approach that focuses only on the child's behavior will not work.

Is your family ready for the challenge? Or perhaps a better question is, Are *you* ready? Take a look at yourself and your responses to your strong-willed child. God gave you a beautiful child, strong will and all, and he has a design in mind for you, your child, and your entire family. At times your family will bond together, and at times you will endure separation that is sad and threatening. But even during separation, God is in charge.

"There is a time for everything, and a season for every activity under heaven: . . . a time to tear down and a time to build, a time to weep and a time to laugh, . . . a time to embrace and a time to refrain" (Eccl. 3:1, 3–5). See the seasons in your family as God-appointed, and allow his grace to see you through your seasons of change.

For Your Consideration

1. How can being overly involved in your family hurt both you and your child?
2. What areas of your life contribute security, meaning, and enjoyment to you personally?

3. Do you take personal responsibility for your own well-being? How?

4. In what ways do your children distract you from dealing with your own fears and insecurities? How do they distract you from taking personal responsibility for your own life?

5. What are some of the major events or circumstances that have disrupted your family or brought a sense of loss?

6. Are you able to let go of worry about your strong-willed child and focus on your life?

7. What person's approval is most important to you? Does this approval keep you from making necessary changes in your own life?

8. Why is emotional separation hard on families?

Skill Builders

Win-win. In family situations, parents often face win-lose conflicts where someone gets his way and another must give up his desires. When possible, work toward win-win situations. In win-win encounters, both the parent and the child work together to find a solution that is considerate to each one. The parent remains the final authority but works on resolving conflict in a mutually respectful way.

For example, Mom and Louis have a scheduling conflict. She has a 3:30 meeting and Louis has soccer practice.

Mom:　"I'll give up my meeting so I can take you to practice! *(Lose-win)*

Louis:　"Never mind. I'll miss practice so you can go to your meeting! *(Lose-win)*

Mom:　"How about having Pete's mom take you today and I'll drive to practice on Friday?" *(Win-win)*

Practice win-win conflict resolution with your children so that you consider everyone's thoughts, feelings, and desires.